D0824721

THE POLITICS OF THE FINANCIAL
SERVICES REVOLUTION

The Politics of the Financial Services Revolution

The USA, UK and Japan

Michael Moran

First published 1991

Published by
MACMILLAN ACADEMIC AND PROFESSIONAL LTD
Houndmills, Basingstoke, Hampshire RG21 2XS
and London
Companies and representatives
throughout the world

Printed and bound in Great Britain by
Antony Rowe Ltd, Chippenham, Wiltshire

10   9   8   7   6   5   4   3
06   05   04   03   02   01   00   99

British Library Cataloguing in Publication Data
Moran Michael, *1946–*
The politics of the financial services revolution : the
USA, UK and Japan.
1. Capitalist countries. Economic activity. Regulation
I. Title
330.9
ISBN 0–333–41562–0

For Liam and Cathy

Contents

Acknowledgements

Colin Crouch and Ronald Dore bear a large responsibility for this book. They began and guided the ESRC 'Corporatism and Accountability' research initiative. Much of the work reported here – especially the Anglo-American part – began life as a study sponsored by that initiative.

From Crouch and Dore, and from the ESRC, I received considerable intellectual stimulation, and substantial financial support. I was lucky enough to be able to pick the brains of Sir Arthur Knight, who was my *rapporteur* on the initiative. I also interviewed regulators and market participants in New York, Washington and London during 1985–86. These interviews were off-the-record, and rarely crop up here as evidence except in an occasional note, but they were vital in clarifying my thoughts at key stages of the work. I am grateful to all the busy people who gave up time to talk to me.

This work is based on documents in the public domain, and to get at them I had the help of many librarians. I particularly wish to thank the staff of: the City Business Library; the Library of the University of Manchester Business School; the City of Manchester Central Reference Library; the Library of the British Museum; the Library of Congress; the Library of the Securities and Exchange Commission; and the New York Public Library.

The quotations at the heads of chapters are from Joseph Schumpeter, *Capitalism, Socialism and Democracy* (original publication 1943; quotations in the University edition, Allen and Unwin, 1976 on pp. 299, 146, 132–3, 138 and 143).

The book was preceded by many papers given in various places, and I used these shamelessly to pillage the ideas of friends and colleagues. I was especially helped by participation in the ECPR workshop on 'Deregulation in Western Europe' at Amsterdam in 1987, and by collaboration with Leigh Hancher in preparing for publication the papers given in the Workshop. Part of the book was written during study leave from my job at Manchester University. I thank the University – and especially my colleagues in the Department of Government – for making this study leave possible. It is a pleasure to thank Karen Hall, who typed the manuscript. I also wish to thank Tony Grahame, my Macmillan copy-editor.

And finally, I thank my family for putting the whole thing in proportion. They have never concealed their view that writing books like this is hardly a suitable activity for a grown man; and their amused scepticism has been a reminder that there is more to life than states and financial markets.

MICHAEL MORAN
Glossop, Derbyshire

1 Corporatism, Regulation and Financial Services

> No responsible person can view with equanimity the consequences
> of extending the democratic method, that is to say the sphere of
> 'politics', to all economic affairs.

1 THE PURPOSE OF THE BOOK

Comparative enquiry resembles foreign travel. Both are expensive, time consuming and bewildering. Both are also best done in a spirit of parochialism. We learn about abroad by comparing foreigners with ourselves. The most rewarding comparison, like the most rewarding travel, thus consists in a continuous series of surprises – sometimes at the strangeness and sometimes at the familiarity of foreign practices.

This book was prompted by surprise, and was written in a spirit of parochialism. I began in the early 1980s trying to reconstruct the politics of the 'Big Bang' in the London financial markets – in other words, trying to understand the constellation of organised interests and public authority which produced the revolutionary changes in regulation and market practices experienced in London after 1983.[1] The surprise lay in the fact that the British economy – long notorious for backwardness and decline – in this instance seemed close to the vanguard of international change. A more detailed examination revealed yet another surprise, this time about the role of the state. The financial services revolution in Britain was shaped by state intervention. The changes of the 1980s happened because state power was used to override those business interests hostile to radical reform in financial markets. Yet not only is Britain conventionally viewed as a country incapable of adapting to world economic change; the state in Britain is widely thought of as a weak, liberal institution, unable to impose its will on powerful sectional interests. In Dyson's words:

> British elite culture displays a reluctance to give leadership, undertake
> development functions or exploit technical knowledge. These deep
> inhibitions about exercising 'public power' are the product in part
> of a liberal ideology that emphasises diffusion of authority . . . There

1

is an addiction to crisis avoidance and group consent rather than the self-confidence that comes from the notion of the indivisible, unitary character of 'public power' and its inherent right to regulate in the general interest.[2]

Yet in 1983 groups at the very apex of the British elite, in the civil service and the Bank of England, intervened to compel revolutionary changes in financial services. Why was the state in this instance a leader of reform? Was it because, contrary to received wisdom, state authority was actually neither weak nor prey to the power of sectional interests? Was it, alternatively, because the state in Britain had indeed been captured by private interests – but private interests demanding revolutionary change? Or was it due to the connections between the British state and other state actors in the world financial system?

These questions could only be answered by comparative enquiry. The changes in London are part of an international revolution – and our experiences have both shaped, and been shaped by, these larger events. The events in question are commonly, and rightly, labelled the world financial services revolution – a set of radical changes undergone in recent years by the banking and securities markets of all advanced capitalist states. Putting the British experience into this comparative setting produces one more striking and perplexing surprise – the examination of which is the chief purpose of this book. In the 1980s 'deregulation' was the most important theme of policy debate in advanced capitalist economies, and its importance was nowhere greater than in the financial services sector. The financial services revolution was commonly treated as synonymous with the 'deregulation' of financial markets; and that word, whatever else it meant, clearly suggested that the state's role in regulation was diminishing. The reality has been otherwise. The British experience has been mirrored elsewhere. The world financial services revolution has not involved retreat by the state. On the contrary: state agencies have been central actors in the revolutionary process; and the revolution in key instances strengthened the hold of the states over financial regulation. Revolutions often have surprising outcomes; but the almost universal contradiction between the images of 'deregulation', and the reality of more state control, obviously demands special attention. The most important purpose of this book is therefore to describe, and if possible to explain, this transformation of the state's role in financial regulation.

A comprehensive comparative study of the politics of financial services revolution would encompass all capitalist economies, because not a single capitalist nation has been untouched by the events in question. It would

TABLE 1   *Comparative size of three largest banking centres, by nation (outstanding lending as percentage share of total market)*

	1975	1985	1989*
United Kingdom	27.1	25.4	20.5
Japan	4.6	10.8	20.6
United States	13.5	13.3	10.0

NOTE: * denotes 1st quarter.
SOURCE: *Bank of England Quarterly Bulletin*, November 1989, p. 518.

cover, for instance, 'the little Big Bang in Paris'; the reorganisation of securities trading in Amsterdam; the attempts in the Federal Republic of Germany to secure 'Finanzplatz Deutschland'; and the reform of trading practices in Canada.[3] The scope of the book is actually more limited. The experiences of Paris, Amsterdam, Frankfurt and Ontario are important. But these are only outposts of revolution. The central locations lie elsewhere: in the United States, the United Kingdom and Japan. It is in these three countries that the largest financial markets, and the largest financial institutions, have primary locations. It is the markets in New York and London that have supplied the greatest engineers of financial innovation. And it is the high diplomacy of financial negotiations between state agencies in America, Britain and Japan that continues to shape the world financial services revolution.

The fact that the book is concerned with the politics of revolution in these three countries dictates the division of the chapters. The United States is the epicentre of revolution. American political and financial might has been the most important influence on the world financial services sector in the post-war years; and the domestic regulatory history of banking and securities has provided the most immediate stimulus to revolutionary change. Both by virtue of wealth and power, and by virtue of its place in the chronicle of the revolution, America deserves first place.

London's significance is different. Britain's native financial services industries, like most other British industries, long ago lost their domination of world markets. Two British banks, true, head the standard ranking of the world's top banks; but they are the only two British institutions in the top twenty, against nine Japanese firms.[4] Yet as Table 1 shows, London is one of the world's leading international banking centres: 'The City', to use its short-hand title, is a great world trading arena in financial services.

It achieved this position because of its attraction to Americans, and it has retained its prominence in recent years because of its attraction to the Japanese: in the 1970s and 1980s British banks commanded only around one-fifth of London's international banking.[5] When American institutions marched into London, American power and American preoccupations marched with them. London is the most important arena through which the American financial services revolution has been exported – both to Britain's own financial system and to those of other major capitalist economies. This is why the chapter on the United Kingdom (Chapter 3) succeeds the examination of the United States (Chapter 2).

The history of American financial power also explains why Japan appears in the study. The Japanese are in some senses laggards in the financial services revolution. At home, Japanese institutions and markets have often been reluctant to embrace the innovations so enthusiastically engineered in London and New York. In another sense, however, Tokyo (and Osaka) hold the key both to the revolutionary changes of the 1980s amd to the way they will unfold for the remaining decade of the century. The astounding success of the Japanese economy makes the domestic market for financial services in Japan one of the richest prizes in world competition. Until now that prize has been almost monopolised by Japanese enterprises. The size of the domestic market has in turn made these enterprises into world giants: for instance, at the end of the 1980s the measures conventionally used to estimate size suggested that the world's biggest stock exchange, insurance firms, banks and securities firms were all Japanese. These giants, we shall see, began in the 1980s to challenge, and in some cases to supplant, American institutions in world markets: by 1988, for instance, the Japanese banks in London were accounting for 36 per cent of an international banking business that had once been dominated by Americans.[6] In brief, Japan is central to the latest stages of the financial services revolution because it is at the heart of the struggle for markets, both its own and those elsewhere.

The analysis offered in these pages marks a shift in the focus of intellectual interest in the study of financial markets. Studies of financial services have hitherto been distinguished by one overriding concern – with the capacity or otherwise of financial markets to deliver credit for investment to the rest of the economy. This issue has dominated policy argument in Britain since the days of the Macmillan Committee, and it continues to shape scholarly accounts. It is the nub, for instance, of Hu's case that the culture of financial markets in Britain is hostile to the long-term financing of industry; of Dore's similar account, based on observation of Japan; of Zysman's argument that the very capacity

to liquidate obsolete investments and make new ones in the industrial
sphere is a function of the way capital markets are organised; and of
Cox's more particular suggestion that bank-dominated markets ensure the
most effective provision of industrial finance.[7]

These concerns, though important, have meant the neglect of more
obvious considerations. We commonly speak of the financial services
sector precisely because, though the boundaries are unclear, it is possible
to identify a range of institutions producing and selling an array of
financial goods and services. In the most advanced capitalist states these
goods and services are to an increasing degree traded internationally, and
their production is dominated by giant multinationals.[8] Firms in financial
services thus resemble those in chemicals, vehicles, pharmaceuticals or any
other important sector: they enter competitive world markets in the hope of
trading profitably in a range of products.

From this elementary observation follow three obvious implications.
First, as in other important industries organised on a multinational scale
there are great differences in the success with which particular firms,
and the industries of individual countries, compete in the marketplace.
Second, the operation of markets is dominated by a ceaseless struggle for
comparative advantage – a struggle between firms, between rival financial
centres and between the industries of whole countries. Finally, and most
important, in this struggle for comparative advantage state agencies are
key actors. In an epoch when the leading capitalist nations have ceased to
compete with each other militarily, the struggle for comparative economic
advantage has become an overriding influence on state policy. In this
struggle the management of the financial services sector is central. It is
central, in part, because of the crucial role of financial markets in serving
the wider economy – an importance attested by the long debate about the
relationship between the organisation of capital markets and the supply of
funds to manufacturing industry. But financial services firms also have a
growing direct importance, as major employers and as generators of foreign
exchange. A comparative advantage in financial services is as important
for employment and prosperity as is a comparative advantage in a central
manufacturing activity like automobiles or chemicals. In Britain in 1989,
for instance, banking, insurance and allied business services employed
over 2.6 million people. Of these, over 780 000 worked in Greater
London alone, itself an increase of over 200 000 in the course of the
1980s.[9] The despised 'City revolution' has, in other words, been a major
creator of jobs, part of the foundation of prosperity in south-east England
– and thus a significant cause of the ascendancy of Thatcherism in British
politics.

A comparative advantage in financial services is therefore a key influence on 'bread and butter' economic management. But it also has a more diffuse significance for governments. One of the most important competitive struggles in the world financial services sector involves the battle for supremacy between different, nationally regulated, financial centres. In Gilpin's words: 'Financial markets tend to be highly centralised and hierarchical in structure because of the importance of economies of scale and pooled information. This creates competition among individual centres to be dominant at the apex of the system'.[10] As the example of London shows, success in this competition can also be a major source of jobs and prosperity. But it also brings the benefits of prestige to state actors who regulate a major international financial centre. In the case of the United Kingdom, for instance, the necessity to defend London's preeminent position was an almost unthinking tenet of public policy in the 1980s. In the transnational hierarchy of financial regulators the Bank of England enjoys, by virtue of London's eminence, a place at the very top – a position quite beyond the normal expectations of the central bank of a declining industrial power with an insignificant world currency. London's importance as an international financial centre offers the state elites of this declining power one of the few remaining opportunities to play a leading international role. Regulating a major financial centre is, for purposes of state prestige, thus like possessing nuclear weapons, or controlling an industry at the leading edge of technology.

In the struggle for comparative advantage states dispose of one critical resource – the system of regulation itself. The extent, form, and purpose of state intervention is the single most important feature of any system of financial regulation; and this system is itself a source of comparative advantage, or of disadvantage. The reforms introduced in London in 1983, for instance, gave London a significant competitive edge over rivals like Frankfurt and Paris. Of course in all economic sectors regulation, by affecting competitive conditions, can in this way influence the balance of advantage. But competitive conditions in financial services are uniquely sensitive to the regulatory arrangements because the 'goods' traded are themselves mostly regulatory creations – contracts, legally binding or otherwise, embodying a structure of financial claims and obligations. In the words of a recent OECD report: 'The legislative and regulative provisions that define the permissible spheres of activity for various institutions operating in the financial services sector determine to a great extent the kind of institutions and the kind of financial services that develop.'[11]

The struggle for comparative advantage is the dominant fact of life in financial markets; systems of regulation are themselves powerful sources of comparative advantage; the single most important feature of a system of regulation is the form and extent of state power in that system. Already we have some clues that will help us solve our most important puzzle – why the supposed age of deregulation is actually an age of growing state management of regulatory change in financial markets. But this is to anticipate. We first need a sketch of financial services, and of the revolutionary changes that have in recent years come over the markets. That is the purpose of Section 2, which readers with any knowledge of the financial services industry may safely skip.

2   THE FINANCIAL SERVICES REVOLUTION: A SKETCH

The financial services revolution is a shorthand expression for a series of important changes in ownership structures and trading practices that have come over the financial services sector in the advanced capitalist world, notably since the early 1970s. Like most industrial classifications, the concept of a 'financial services sector' is a mixture of political shorthand and analytical convenience. It encompasses a series of markets, connected to each other by varying degrees of closeness. Some of these markets are small and confined within nations; others are huge, truly global systems. The customers range from the humblest saver with a few pounds in a building society, to sovereign states or multinational corporations raising debt on the international capital markets. In the 1980s the industry became widely identified in the public mind with one activity, trading in financial instruments – an identification strengthened by scandals such as the Boesky affair, and fictional representations in plays like *Serious Money* and films like *Wall Street*.[12] This image of financial markets as gambling arenas has recently been expressed in a devastating critique by Strange:

> The Western financial system is rapidly coming to resemble nothing as much as a vast casino. Every day games are played in this casino that involve sums of money so large that they cannot be imagined. At night the games go on at the other side of the world. In the towering office blocks that dominate all the great cities of the world, rooms are full of chain-smoking young men all playing these games. Their eyes are fixed on the computer screens flickering with changing prices. They play by intercontinental telephone or by tapping electronic machines. They are just like gamblers in casinos watching the clicking spin of a silver ball on a roulette wheel and putting their chips on red or black, odd numbers or even ones.[13]

The casino aspects of the industry were indeed central to its changing character in the 1970s and 1980s, but trading of this sort is only one of a wide range of activities encompassed in the phrase 'financial services'. A financial market is best pictured as a social arena where three things are exchanged. First, contracts, in the form of financial instruments like bonds or equities, which specify a range of claims and obligations between buyers and sellers. Second, information: for instance, real time data about prices; economic intelligence packaged in a wide range of formats; specialised information about such matters as the legal conditions governing particular trading activities. Third, and finally, commercial services: these include insurance and related kinds of risk management, accounting and auditing, broking, and the provision of advice to investors.[14]

This sketch makes clear some obvious features of the financial services sector. It is far more diverse, both in institutional structure and trading practices, than is suggested by the common identification with the frenetic life of trading rooms. It is a major supplier of services to other sectors and is itself a significant customer – for instance, of the telecommunications industries.

The acknowledged heart of the financial services sector lies in the banking and securities industries. It is conventional to make a distinction between commercial and investment banking. The former covers taking deposits, making loans, providing the money and credit transmission services that are vital to a complex economy. The central function of investment banking is raising corporate finance. In some systems (for example, the United States and Japan) the law largely prohibits the same institutions from engaging in commercial and investment banking; in others (most famously Germany) there prevails a system of universal banking where the same institutions provide the full range of banking services. Investment banking is in turn closely connected to the issuing and trading of securities. In Anglo-American minds securities markets organised on stock exchanges are thought to be key mechanisms for providing corporate finance, through the issue and trading of equity in companies. But in the most successful post-war capitalist economies – Japan and West Germany – bank credit has been the chief source of industrial finance, while in the Anglo-American system the largest national securities markets have actually been in bonds funding public debt, rather than in company equities.[15] Indeed, the biggest single domestic securities market in the world – for United States government securities – is not even organised on a stock exchange.[16]

The various parts of the banking and securities industries have developed different institutional structures in different nations. The simplest summary of the financial services revolution is that it consists of a growing similarity between the institutional structures and trading practices in the financial markets of all the major capitalist economies. The competitive histories of commercial and investment banking lie at the heart of this growing similarity. Banking played a central role in the development of capitalism. The great finance capitalists of New York and London in the later decades of the nineteenth century were crucial agents in opening new markets and in the consequent creation, for the first time in history, of a truly world economic system. (This pioneering rôle was reflected in the way so many of the business empires of the great finance capitalists were also linked to railways and to shipping.) Up to the First World War a large part of the financial services sector consisted of aggressively competitive firms – notably American concerns – operating on an international scale. Investment banking was highly cosmopolitan; in Britain, of the elite merchant banks at the outbreak of the Great War, over half were German in origin.[17]

The twin catastrophes of the First World War and the Great Depression destroyed much of the open international economic system which the finance capitalists had helped regulate. Markets became more restrictive in their business practices and less international in operation. Public policy became strongly nationalistic. Few states permitted foreign takeovers of domestic financial services firms, and most put prohibitions, or high barriers, against foreign participation in domestic banking and securities markets. Domestic competitive struggles were also severely controlled. Entry to securities markets and to banking markets was commonly restricted, either by law, by a customary exercise of public power (the position in England before the Banking Act of 1979) or by cartels in the markets themselves. Likewise, inside the markets there were restrictions on price competition (for example, by minimum commission rates in brokerage business, and by ceilings on interest rates for bank loans and deposits); on competition through product innovation; and on competition through acquisition.[18] Financial innovation was discouraged on the grounds that novel financial instruments, and novel methods of salesmanship, endangered financial prudence and stability. From the outbreak of the First World War, until the 1950s, the characteristic features of financial markets were restrictions on competition and hostility to product innovation. The financial services sector was a backwater of capitalism.

The financial services revolution is transforming this backwater. Four features of revolutionary change merit notice. For clarity they are first listed here.

1. Intensified competition, involving the destruction of barriers to price competition and to market entry.
2. Rapid spurts of innovation, partly involving the adaptation of new technology to create new patterns of trading.
3. Changes in the structure of ownership, leading to the growing domination of markets by multinational corporations.
4. Increasing international integration of the largest financial markets, and the creation of a global system of trading dominated by a small number of competing financial centres.

Two examples illustrate the rise of price competition. First, there has occurred a wholesale dismantling of controls over interest rates in the banking industry. The most notable example has been the phasing out of statutory ceilings on rates to lenders in US banking markets, thus encouraging more aggressive competition for custom.[19] Second, price controls have been abolished in the securities brokerage industry on both sides of the Atlantic. 'Minimum commissions' on bargains transacted for customers were first relaxed, and then phased out in New York after 1975 and in London after 1983.[20] The end of restrictions on price competition, though it attracted great public attention, was less important in itself than as a sign of more fundamental changes in the competitive structure of financial services. The end of price restrictions was usually accompanied by, and in many cases accelerated, pressure to dismantle restrictions on entry. The 'old' financial services sector was characterised by significant barriers to entry and by the segregation of institutions in different markets. The barriers to entry to markets have on both sides of the Atlantic either been dismantled or circumvented. Banks have, in various guises, moved into new markets, such as securities and housing finance; at the same time securities firms, and other institutions, have begun competing in traditional banking markets.[21] These changes have themselves signalled a wider cultural and institutional alteration, for they mark an intensification of competition – between firms, between different sections of the industry and between financial centres.

There is in turn an intimate connection between intensified competition and the drive for innovation, because the creation of new financial instruments or trading practices is one of the most effective ways of securing a competitive advantage. In American commercial banking in the late 1970s, for instance, there was ferocious competition to invent new kinds of savings accounts which could circumvent prohibitions on the payment of interest to depositors. In investment banking in the 1980s the search for new modes of attack and defence in takeovers was a major form of struggle between firms. Competition through contractual innovation, depending essentially on the ingenuity of lawyers and accountants, has been a key force for change in financial services. Some innovation has also exploited the latest available electronic technology. In the American securities industry, for instance, challenges to the domination of traditional 'stock exchanges' have been mounted using telecommunications technology to create electronic alternatives to traditional trading on exchange 'floors'.[22] Innovation is nevertheless dependent less on technology than on institutional flexibility and human ingenuity. The most important kind of innovation in markets lies in the adaptation and creation of financial instruments; in other words in the creation of contracts. The pace of innovation is thus fixed, not so much by technology, as by the perceived rewards of innovation, and by the ingenuity of the professionals, like lawyers and accountants, in dreaming up new contractual creations.

In recent decades this ingenuity has stretched beyond the invention of particular contracts to the creation of whole markets. Two of the most dynamic are those in financial derivatives and in Eurocurrencies. The best known derivatives are financial futures – contracts to exchange a financial instrument (for instance, a bond or equity) at some future date at an agreed price. Futures contracts now exist for most financial instruments.[23] The boom in futures transactions began in the United States in the mid-1970s, and has now spread to most important financial centres: LIFFE (the London International Financial Futures Exchange) was established in 1982, and a financial futures exchange was set up in Tokyo in 1989. The Euromarkets deal in financial instruments denominated in currencies held outside their country of issue. The original (and still most important) Eurocurrency was the dollar held by banks in London; but the Euromarkets now extend to yen traded in New York or German marks traded in London.[24]

The significance of the Euromarkets lies partly in their size and in the rapidity of their growth.[25] But they are also significant because they are at the heart of regulatory change in financial services. The single most important force creating and sustaining these markets has been the opportunities they offer to escape regulatory restrictions prevailing in the country of origin of the individual currencies. The original Eurodollar market grew because holders of Eurodollar deposits could escape taxes and limits on interest rates imposed on holders of domestic dollar deposits. Indeed, one of the chief continuing attraction of Eurobonds is that they are commonly issued in a form offering holders the chance to avoid (or even evade) taxation. The firms active in the market have also been regulatory pioneers. American and Japanese institutions, for instance, have used their Euromarket operations in London to break the barriers (like those separating commercial from investment banks) that exist in their native regulatory regimes.[26]

Euromarkets and markets in financial futures illustrate two major features of the financial services revolution: intensified competition and rapid innovation. But the Euromarkets, dominated as they are by large institutions, also illuminate a third major aspect: transformations in the structure of ownership. On both sides of the Atlantic control of firms has increasingly shifted from partnerships to corporate hierarchies. In London, for instance, the disappearance of the largest stock broking partnerships into multinational giants was one of the most important developments of the 1980s. There has been a corresponding growth in the size of firms, an expansion across national boundaries and – wherever the rules allow or can be circumvented – an expansion across a wide range of financial markets. Multinational financial conglomerates operating in different sectors of the financial services industry are nothing new; but the financial services revolution involves the increasing domination of the most important markets by the multinational giants. The centre of gravity in the industry has thus shifted towards giant firms. These giants are among the most important agents of structural change – aggressively challenging regulatory boundaries, ownership structures and competitive practices.

The rise of the multinational giant in financial services is itself linked to the fourth and final feature of change in financial services. In Strange's words, nowadays 'markets are predominantly global, while the authorities are predominantly national'.[27] Many forces are encouraging this process of global integration. The dismantling of foreign exchange controls in key states (Britain in 1979, Japan in 1980) encouraged international diversification by investors: in 1980, for instance, Japanese investors bought $1 billion of American equities; by 1987 the figure was estimated at $12 billion.[28] This conscious process of international diversification is in turn assisted by the more impersonal forces of technology, whose advance 'has made distance, unfamiliarity with other economic environments, and different (national) methods of trading increasingly less important'.[29]

The growing global integration of the financial services industries is itself a part of a wider structural shift. The most rapid recent growths in international economic exchange have been in service sectors – tourism, advertising, consultancy, data provision services and, of course, banking and securities.[30] Securing and exploiting a comparative advantage in services is now a key to successful economic management. In financial services there are two important kinds of comparative advantage – those enjoyed by firms, and those enjoyed by locations. The two do not always go together. The importance of Tokyo and New York as world financial centres is indeed plainly due in large part to the underlying might of their national economies and to the financial services firms produced by those economies. But London's comparative advantage as a world financial centre is due, above all, to regulatory policy: to, for instance, the conscious decision to encourage the development of the Euromarkets in Britain and to the equally conscious decision to reconstruct the whole system after 1983.[31] In the world financial services revolution – the intensifying struggles for comparative advantage, the constant drives for innovation, the changes in ownership structures, and the global integration of markets – the participation of state institutions in the regulatory system is thus a key factor. Appropriately, therefore, the character of regulatory systems is our next concern.

3 CORPORATISM, BUSINESS REGULATION AND FINANCIAL CHANGE

The financial services revolution has an economic face, but it also has a political face. It amounts to more than a set of changes in ownership structures, and trading practices; it also involves a series of changes in the rules governing those structures and practices. In brief, it is a revolution in *regulation*.

The character of that revolution – and the essential argument of the succeeding chapters – can be summarised as follows. The regulation of financial services in the most advanced capitalist economies shows a marked bias to corporatism. The revolution in regulation involves the reconstruction of corporatism along similar lines in different economies: increasing codification of rules; a more prominent role for formally constituted organisations, both public and private; and the growing penetration of law into the regulatory system. A summary description of the regulatory face of the financial services revolution is therefore as follows: it involves the growing *codification, institutionalisation and juridification* of corporatist arrangements. By more codification I simply mean that rules are becoming more elaborate, and are more likely to be written down than to rest on informal understandings. By more institutionalisation I mean that organisations devoted to the regulatory task are growing in importance: they are acquiring more authority and more resources. Juridification I treat as a special kind of codification: it involves putting the rules onto the statute book and settling disputes about those rules in the courts.

Explaining the origins of this argument obviously has to start with a consideration of 'corporatism', an idea whose recent intellectual history is fortunately now well known. The first wave of modern corporatist theorists in the 1970s differed on many issues, but they were united in picturing corporatism as a form of partnership or control linking the national representatives of capital and labour with the state.[32] These visions of 'macro-corporatism' had hardly been elaborated when they were overtaken by events. By the end of the 1970s the power of organised labour was in decline on both sides of the Atlantic, while ideologies of deregulation and market economics were in the ascendant. Reaganism and Thatcherism made the idea of corporatist economic management seem a fantasy.[33] A second wave of corporatist literature thus began addressing the problem of Anglo-American 'exceptionalism' – trying to solve the puzzle of corporatism's apparent failure to become established in the Anglo-American world. The crest of this second wave was marked by Katzenstein's work, which argued that corporatist economic management was itself exceptional. It was typical of a collection of small European states, where it had been produced by twin forces: by the response to the economic and political crises of the 1930s and 1940s; and by a continuing sense of vulnerability felt by small nations in big world markets.[34]

Over a decade after the initial revival of interest in the study of corporatism there is common ground that corporatism as a form of economic management is, far from being the wave of the future, a fairly rare phenomenon. Yet corporatist theory retains its power because it helps make sense of a regulatory pattern that is ubiquitous in market economies. In the regulation of sectors and industries there is, to use Offe's words, a widespread 'attribution of public status to interest groups'.[35] Regulation is, characteristically, a public function done by private interests. This recognition has produced a third wave of literature, concerned with corporatist arrangements at the sectoral, or meso, level. As Cawson put it:

> Meso-corporatism refers to the fusion of the processes of interest representation, decision-making and policy implementation with respect to a more restricted range of issues than the 'system-steering' concerns of macro-corporatism. There is no presumption that meso-corporatist arrangements are tripartite in form, or that the interests they embrace are restricted to capital and labour. The range of collective actors which enter into meso-corporatist political exchanges with state actors includes trade unions and sectoral associations of business interests.[36]

It is possible, as some have argued, that employing 'corporatism' to describe this state of affairs is a misuse of the original word.[37] Indeed, some of those who have documented meso-corporatism in the regulation of American business life, like Lowi and Wolfe, reject the term.[38] But meso-corporatism catches key features of arrangements at the sectoral level: the appropriation of a regulatory role by private interests; the transformation of private, voluntary associations into authoritative bodies; the restriction of political and economic competition. It may be that a better word can describe what we now call meso-corporatism, but it has yet to be coined. No other notion makes better sense, we shall see, of regulation in financial services. The story of the financial services revolution is, to put it simply, a tale of the way crises of meso-corporatist regulation have compelled growing state intervention in the regulatory system.

There exists a bias to meso-corporatism in financial services for the same reasons that explain a meso-corporatist bias in business regulation generally. In nations uniting democratic politics with market economics business interests simultaneously face great dangers and enjoy great privileges. The dangers come from the tensions between, on the one hand, the presumptive equality of a political order offering equal and universal rights of citizenship and, on the other, actual inequalities of the market. The privileged position of business comes from the ascendancy of business ideology, and the fact that firms have the greatest share of the resources – money, knowledge, personnel – needed to make regulation work. In Lindblom's words:

> Corporate executives in all private enterprise systems . . . decide a nation's industrial technology, the pattern of work organisation, location of industry, market structure, resource allocation and, of course, executive compensation and status . . . In short, in any private enterprise system, a large category of major decisions is turned over to businessmen, both small and large.[39]

The bias to meso-corporatism marks a compromise struck between demands to regulate private power and wealth, and the needs of privileged private interests to have protection against democratic politics. The political function of the arrangement has been expressed exactly by Cawson: 'the recognition of relatively privileged categories of interest within corporatist relationships has either created new hierarchies or licensed existing ones, and this has undermined the universality of citizenship and transformed the democratic character of the state.'[40]

The image of 'bias' used here is exactly that offered in Middlemas's study of corporatism in Britain. The tendency for regulation to drift to meso-corporatism resembles the 'bias' of a wood in the game of bowls, which will drag in a particular direction unless corrected.[41] In financial services the extent and form of that bias is a function of a range of forces – and since their examination shapes the individual case studies of the three countries it is as well to sketch them here. They are: national setting, institutional structures and historical crises.

The first is obvious: regulation is deeply influenced by the national institutional setting in which it occurs. 'Each nation's business community', writes Vogel, 'has experienced the kind of regulation it deserves.'[42] There are distinctive national ways of going about the job of regulating private economic power. The United States is a country where public authority is fragmented and where courtrooms are central arenas of political and economic struggle. It accomplishes regulation through an immensely complex series of statutes administered, often in a furiously adversarial atmosphere, by an organisational network of breath-taking complexity. In Britain financial elites established a regulatory order largely separate from the central institutions of the state, and regulation was chiefly done by an informally organised elite, with hardly any reference to the statute book. In Japan, a society averse to litigation, and ruled by an elite fused together at the top of party politics, the bureaucracy and the business community, regulatory struggles are fought over between different institutional fragments of the elite, and when settled are embodied in 'administrative guidance' rather than in law.[43]

These trivial observations illustrate a second central feature of the regulatory process: the detailed institutional arrangements matter a great deal. Hall has systematically identified why this is so: because the interests at work are necessarily articulated through institutional structures; because the making of policy is 'invariably a collective endeavour', and institutional structures determine how the collective activity happens; and because implementation is the vital condition for the realisation of policy, and implementation only happens through, and is shaped by, institutional structures.[44] The extent and form of any bias to corporatism is thus heavily influenced by the institutional setting – and this is why here each chapter on the separate nations begins with a description of the institutional structure of financial regulation.

The institutional structure that directs and redirects the bias to corporatism is itself, of course, a product of wider historical forces. Regulatory systems are paradigms of institutional life in general: in other words, their existence consists of periods of routine punctuated by crises. Indeed, regulatory regimes are characteristically created by crises: in the American case, to take only the most obvious example, financial services regulation is still indelibly marked by the experiences following the Wall Street Crash of 1929. The way a system of regulation works is thus only in part a function of its present structure, and of the way that structure helps create and sustain coalitions of interest; it is also a function of the historical crisis which caused its conception. The features of that crisis remain inscribed in the regulatory structure decades after the original events have passed away, and the original protagonists are dead and buried. That is why each of the succeeding chapters on individual countries contains an examination of the origins and evolution of the national regulatory regime.

The sceptical reader might now wonder what is left of the innate bias to meso-corporatism if regulatory regimes can be so influenced by particular national institutions and contingent historical episodes The answer lies partly in the succeeding chapters, which for all the intervening influences still show that the bias powerfully exists, and that there is a common drift towards more codification, formal organisation and juridification. But the answer also lies in more general observations, and these influence the organisation of later chapters. The countries examined here share three features: the experience of structural change in financial markets; the existence of democratic institutions that are in tension with corporatist arrangements; and common membership of an international political and economic order which shapes the domestic policy. We consider each in turn.

The financial services revolution is an episode involving structural change in the pursuit of competitive advantage. Alterations in the structure of markets inevitably create changes in the nature of the interests clamouring for representation. Old established firms decline or, revitalised, try to enter new markets; groups of firms are born; whole new markets – in Eurocurrencies and in financial derivatives – are created, and grow to major economic importance. The settled hierarchy of privileged interests that meso-corporatism creates is thus challenged. The consensus supporting corporatist practices collapses: the privileged fall out with each other, as they see the chance of forming alliances with new interests and of creating new privileges. The sections on 'the politics of structural change' in each of the three country case-studies are designed to substantiate the general proposition that rapid structural changes at the heart of the financial services revolution have caused crises of this kind in meso-corporatist regulation.

One consequence of these crises has been to heighten the tension between meso-corporatist practices and the wider institutions of pluralist democracy. This tension always exists because corporatist regulation attempts to appropriate the public authority and legitimacy of a democratic state, while restricting, in Cawson's phrase, 'the universality of citizenship'.[45] It is plain that pluralist democracy and meso-corporatism can coexist, but this coexistence demands considerable ideological mystification. The most widespread and successful form of mystification is supplied by ideologies of self-regulation. These ideologies picture the task of regulating markets as a delicate and mysterious business requiring the special skills of practitioners – businessmen and their servants. The agents and institutions of the democratic state are in this way excluded from the detailed activity of regulation.[46] The crisis of meso-corporatism caused by structural change seriously endangers these arrangements. As the consensus supporting corporatism collapses, regulation becomes 'politicised'. The established actors – giant firms, interest groups, formally constituted self-regulatory bodies, bureaucratic fragments of the state – begin forging alliances across the political system: in political parties, legislatures, and in other state agencies. This weakens one of the most important conditions of successful ideological mystification – that the regulatory world be insulated from democratic pluralism. This insulation is necessary because pluralist democracy contains powerful agents of demystification. To put the point more concretely: once financial regulation is 'politicised' there exist numerous individuals and institutions ready to seize on any regulatory failure in order to ask awkward questions about the practical effectiveness of self-regulation. These awkward actors include the characteristic figures of pluralist democracy: policy entrepreneurs of all kinds; ambitious politicians; enquiring reporters; and state agencies ambitious to shape policy and to invade new spheres of jurisdiction. The more open and pluralist the political system, the greater the danger to the mystifying power of ideology and to the privileges of the meso-corporatist order. Of our three countries the United States has the most open, pluralist political arrangements; and it is in the United States, we shall see, that the demystification of business ideology and challenges to meso-corporatist privileges are strongest. Any of a number of issues – regulation of takeovers, investor protection, the control of fraud – would illustrate this process.[47] In the next three chapters the case studies of the politics of 'insider trading' do the job. I chose insider trading because the moral panics over insider dealing show with particular clarity how entanglement with the wider institutions of pluralist democracy is a source of scandal and crisis, and is pushing meso-corporatism towards greater codification, institutionalisation and juridification.

The reader who perseveres to the end of Chapter 2 will find all the themes outlined here illustrated and elaborated: the nature of the bias to meso-corporatism; the way that bias is shaped by national institutional patterns and by the legacy of historical crises; how the crisis of corporatism is caused by structural change; and the exact manner by which entanglement with pluralist democracy creates scandalous revelations and a pressure for a more formally organised and juridified system of corporatism. The final theme – the significance of international economic and political hierarchies for regulatory change – takes longer to emerge, but is central to the Japanese case and to the general account offered in Chapter 5. The significance of the global environment has been well expressed by Ikenberry: 'States participate in both domestic and international political economic systems', he writes. 'Constituted of different organisational capacities and styles of manoeuvre, [they] occupy a unique position to mediate internal and external change.'[48]

The necessity of mediation is made especially urgent by the character of the financial services revolution – which, in its most developed aspects, is a struggle for comparative advantage on a global scale. The actors involved – whether firms or state agencies – have unequal power, and engage in the struggle with unequal success. The most distinctive feature of the international system for most of the post-war years was American domination. In financial services the United States had the richest markets and the biggest institutions. This domination was, of course, only part of a larger system of American power – in the world monetary system and in the military sphere. American dominance, and recent challenges to that dominance, are vital to understanding one of the most striking features of regulation in financial services in different countries – that there exists not only a common bias to meso-corporatism, but a common tendency for systems to drift to more codification, formal organisation and juridification. This drift is in large measure due to the diffusion of American influences to other systems. The changing nature of meso-corporatist regulation is in important respects the results of pressure from an American-dominated international order, and not merely the result of independently generated domestic pressures in separate nations. Among the chief agencies of diffusion have been the institutions of the American state. The reason for the American state's key role lies in another well-known characteristic of the international economic system: the recent challenge to established American supremacy, notably from the astounding success of the Japanese economy. In the 1980s the rise of the Japanese intensified the global struggle for markets, and led to a financial services trade war.[49] To anticipate part of Chapters 4 and 5: for much of the decade one of the key forces at work was a highly instrumental and unstable alliance between American state agencies, like the Treasury, responsible for funding the almost uncontrollable Federal budget deficit, and large Japanese institutions searching for markets in which to invest the fabulous wealth created by the continuing Japanese economic miracle.[50] The creation of these linkages at the international level has, we shall see, been vital to the diffusion of common regulatory practices and structures.

4 CONCLUSION

We began in perplexity, the origin of which was the startling sight of Britain apparently at the forefront of change in an important economic sector, and the even more startling sight of parts of the British state intervening to suppress powerful domestic business interests which were obstructing change. Numerous clues exist to help us decipher this puzzling state of affairs, but they mostly lie in foreign parts. Hence the necessity of a comparative enquiry. There exists a world-wide financial services revolution. British firms are for the most part only minor actors, but London as a financial centre is the cockpit of revolution. The vital changes involve an intensified competitive struggle in markets – the destruction of limits to price competition, the dismantling of barriers between different kinds of markets, the growing domination of multinational firms, the proliferation of financial innovations, and the magnification of competitive struggles onto a global scale.

These revolutionary processes are being superimposed on national regulatory systems already marked by a powerful bias to meso-corporatism. Domestic state structures are fragmented, and the individual fragments are joined in complex networks to private interests. The key fact about meso-corporatism is that, within a pluralist democracy, it confers privileges on private interests. The financial services revolution, by creating new interests and changing the character of those already established, disturbs the fragile consensus on which meso-corporatism rests. This disturbance is partly visible as 'politicisation' – the intrusion into meso-corporatist networks by the agencies of pluralist democracy. More important still it is visible in the creation of new, cross-national networks that have facilitated the diffusion of regulatory practices from the most important actor in the international system, the United States.

The conclusion is obvious: we should now examine the American experience.

2 The United States: Meso-corporatism and Industrial Change

> Capitalism inevitably and by virtue of the very logic of its civilization creates, educates and subsidises a vested interest in social unrest.

1 INTRODUCTION

For much of the post-war period the United States had the most innovative and powerful financial markets in the world. American institutions have been in the forefront of the struggle for comparative advantage, and American financial markets have been among the richest prizes in that struggle. Understanding the politics of the financial services revolution therefore demands, above all, that we analyse the American case.

The organisation of what follows obeys the principles described in Chapter 1. Section 2 sketches the institutional structure of regulation; Section 3 outlines the historical conditions shaping that structure, and the way it has evolved. These sections are more than background, though they are indeed partly designed to acquaint the reader with the outlines and origins of the system. The way a state and an industry adapt to – and in this case facilitate – structural change is in substantial measure a function of institutional hierarchies. Section 2 is thus critical to our understanding. Section 3 explores key variables outlined in the opening chapter – the character and timing of the crises that created the system, and the nature of the American bias to corporatism. Sections 4 and 5 contain the gist of the argument about America. This is that the financial services revolution in the United States amounts to a crisis of meso-corporatism.

The institutions created in the 1930s to regulate financial services could not, by the 1970s, cope with the consequences of competitive struggles. Both the revolution in competitive practices, and the 'scandal' of insider dealing, are a reflection of this crisis. The meso-corporatist system created in the 1930s amounted to a licence in self-regulation granted by the state to powerful private interests. The crisis of the 1970s forced a continuing

21

revision of the terms of that licence.[1] This revision is creating a more elaborately codified and hierarchical structure, in which the freedom to practise self-regulation has been sharply reduced.

2   THE INSTITUTIONS OF MESO-CORPORATISM

All regulatory systems are political creations, and all are in some degree marked by institutional fragmentation. The American financial services sector is nevertheless distinguished by the quite unique degree to which regulation is both politicised and fragmented.

This pattern is in part due to the wider political system: to the federal structure, which distributes authority between the government in Washington and the individual states; to the separation of powers at the Federal level, which divides control of the regulatory process between the three arms of government; and to the elaborate division of administrative labour between different agencies inside the federal executive. The American system thus creates a wide range of competing institutional actors playing overlapping and competing roles in the regulatory system.[2]

This pattern is faithfully reflected in the regulation of the financial services industry: 'regulatory jurisdiction over financial markets is exercised by 10 Federal agencies, at least 50 state agencies, and over 20 self-regulatory organizations.'[3] The individual states play a key part in regulating insurance companies and banks.[4] At the federal level the two most important agencies are the Securities and Exchange Commission (SEC), a federal agency, established under the Securities Exchange Act of 1934; and the Federal Reserve, originally established in 1913. The SEC has two chief responsibilities that put it at the heart of regulatory politics: it supervises the 'disclosure' requirements which are mandatory on the issues of new securities; and it supervises the 'self-regulatory organisations' (principally stock exchanges) which in turn are responsible for the operation of many of the most important securities markets.[5] The Federal Reserve is the American 'central bank' and, like the US Government itself, is federal in character.[6] Its district banks themselves have major regulatory responsibilities. Thus, the Federal Reserve Bank of New York licenses the primary dealers in the US Treasury Bond market, the single most important American securities market.[7]

Although the Federal Reserve's responsibilities for monetary policy mean that it plays an important role in the regulation of the commercial banking system, the major federal responsibility for chartering and inspection is shared between the Comptroller of the Currency – an Office of the US Treasury – and the Federal Deposit Insurance Corporation.[8] The former is the oldest of the regulatory agencies, dating from 1863. The FDIC is part of a family of agencies dating from the New Deal reforms that were prompted by the Great Depression and the associated banking crisis.[9]

An already complex institutional structure has been made more elaborate still by financial innovation. Thus the emergence of markets in financial futures led in the 1970s to the reorganisation of regulation under a Federal Agency (the Commodity Futures Trading Commission), which licenses exchanges as self-regulatory organisations.[10] But futures regulation also reveals a further complicating feature of the American institutional structure. Regulatory jurisdiction is not only divided between a large group of formally constituted Federal agencies; it is also extensively distributed in a network of self-regulatory organisations (SROs). The most obvious cases are the various exchanges that function as SROs licensed by particular agencies. The Securities and Exchange Commission licenses as self-regulatory organisations ten stock exchanges, and licenses also the National Association of Securities Dealers, which regulates the 'over the counter' market. The Commodity Futures Trading Commission licenses thirteen exchanges, and a National Futures Association.[11] In other words, the formal organisation of regulation shows, in key areas of financial services, a conscious bias to meso-corporatism. The bias also reveals itself in less formal aspects of the institutional structure. As we saw earlier, the primary market in Treasury bonds, perhaps the single most important financial market of any kind in the United States, is regulated by informal arrangements conducted through the Federal Reserve Bank of New York. But there is a deeper sense still in which the institutional structure of regulation crosses the divide into what is formally known as the 'private' sector. American financial regulation is guided by the principle of chartering – in other words, firms have historically been conceived to be private institutions performing public functions, and through a charter they acquire a structure of rights and duties.[12] The centrality of firms to the institutional structure is reinforced by the degree to which the major markets are dominated by a small number of firms: in investment banking for instance, the five largest underwriters of domestic corporate debt account for over 70 per cent of the market, and the five largest underwriters of commercial paper have a 90 per cent share.[13]

This elaborate institutional structure is matched by an equally elaborate framework of rules derived from statute. Law, and regulations made with the power of law, are central to the functioning of American financial markets. Among the main landmarks have been the National Bank Act, which first established a system of chartering by Federal Government, during the Civil War; the Federal Reserve Act of 1913, which gave the country a central bank for the first time; the McFadden Act of 1927, which still governs the creation of branch networks in banking; and the Banking Acts of 1933 and 1935, which enforced changes in ownership structures, set up a system of compulsory deposit insurance administered by a federal agency and reorganised the Federal Reserve system.

This elaborate structure of rules has two further institutional consequences. First, it makes Congress a potentially important arena in the struggles over regulation. This is not only – or even chiefly – because of Congress's activity as a legislator; it is because the potential capacity to legislate, coupled with Congressional oversight of the executive agencies, makes the legislature a key place of struggle between the competing interests in the financial services industry. Second, it makes the courts a central arena of struggle. The complexity of the law, its resulting uncertainties, and the sheer difficulty of securing any legislative change through Congress, have given the courts a vital importance. For individual firms, and for whole industries like banking and securities, the battle for comparative advantage in the markets is commonly fought through the courts. The law has thus been one of the main means of controlling competition in financial services. Until well into the 1980s there were significant legal barriers to price competition, in the form of regulatory controls over interest rates.[14] Barriers to market entry include the separation of commercial from investment banking in the Glass-Steagall Act, and the residual limits to the creation of inter-state bank branch networks in the McFadden Act. For over two decades it has therefore been recognised that one of the keys to success in the competitive struggle is success in the courtroom: the firm or industry which succeeds in convincing a judge that a novel financial instrument does not breach a legal prohibition immediately secures a significant competitive advantage.

The importance attached to the reinterpretation and detailed implementation of rules is emphasised by one of the acknowledged features of Congress. The crisis produced by the Wall Street Crash and the Depression resulted, between 1933 and 1935, in a radical and comprehensive overhaul of regulation. But since then decision making has been incremental.[15] There exists no single institution capable of deciding on, and carrying out, wholesale reform. The structure of the American Congress is better geared to obstructing than to passing radical legislative proposals. The competing interests in the financial services industries, and their competing allies in the regulatory agencies, have taken full advantage of this fact. The legislative framework has, in key respects, barely altered in more than half a century, while the structure of markets and the substance of regulation have both changed profoundly. Important developments have indeed happened, but they have typically occurred by persuading the courts and the regulators incrementally to reinterpret and reassess the meaning of existing statutes.

In a world where the formal legal framework is largely fixed because legislation is so difficult to enact, there is a premium on circumventing the regulations or on persuading the appropriate regulatory authority or the courts to interpret the law in a new way. A firm that can invent a financial instrument, or a corporate form, allowing it to compete in a new way, or allowing it to enter a previously forbidden market, thus gains a significant competitive advantage. It reinforces this advantage if at the same time it can control the regulatory order in such a way as to preserve its own traditional domain from entry by predators. Regulatory struggles and competitive struggles are thus entwined. In the words of a Chairman of the Securities and Exchange Commission: 'competitive advantages increasingly turn on regulatory classifications rather than on the economic merits of financial products and services.'[16]

But the institutional structure is given added significance by another consideration: regulatory struggles are themselves closely bound up with competition between agencies. Three considerations shape agency behaviour in these competitive struggles: the effect of regulatory change on their standard operating procedures; the way financial innovation and regulatory adaptation affect agency jurisdiction and prestige; and the extent to which ideologies of cooperative regulation lead those who control agencies to picture themselves as defenders of the interest of 'their' part of the financial services sector. I examine these three factors in turn.

Regulatory agencies in financial services, like those elsewhere in the American system, are bureaucratic institutions burdened with complex tasks.[17] They function through standard operating procedures – uniform procedural and substantive guidelines that ensure coordination and consistency in organisational behaviour. Changes in markets have major, usually disturbing, implications for these standard operating procedures. In banking, to take only the most obvious example, some of the key measures of capital and liquidity adequacy have had to be rethought as a result of innovations that changed the kinds of firms involved in banking markets, and the kinds of markets that conventional banks entered. The need to maintain the effectiveness of standard operating procedure does not always mean that agencies oppose change; on the contrary they often support it because uncontrolled adaptation in markets endangers the effectiveness of their procedures. Thus the Federal Reserve was an enthusiastic supporter of the Depository Institutions Deregulation and Monetary Control Act of

1980 because the law extended the range of institutions for whom the Fed set reserve requirements, thus reversing a long-term loss of membership to the Federal Reserve system.[18]

'Standard operating procedures' are a major feature of the life of complex organisations. A second feature is the drive to defend – and if possible expand – agency jurisdiction. The defence of agency 'turf' is a central, well documented value of organisational life in the American federal system. It is part of the heart of 'bureaucratic politics' and is one of the most important influences on the definition of organisational roles.[19] In financial services, as in other spheres of regulation, market innovations and potential regulatory adaptations are habitually viewed in terms of their implications for agency jurisdiction.

Perhaps the most striking instance of this in recent years is provided by innovations in the markets for 'derivative' financial instruments, like options and futures. The agency responsible for regulating futures, the Commodity Futures Trading Commission, has had major jurisdictional disputes with the Federal Reserve (over regulation of futures dealings in federal government securities) and with the Securities and Exchange Commission (over stock options and stock index futures).[20] Settling these jurisdictional disputes has in turn magnified the complexity of the regulatory system. For example, the Accord that settled the SEC/CFTC dispute gave to the SEC the power to approve new futures contracts in stock indexes, but gave the CFTC regulatory jurisdiction over them once approval was granted.[21]

This urge to defend institutional territory is reinforced by a third feature of the life of regulatory institutions. American financial regulation is largely cooperative regulation. (In this respect it is strikingly different from the adversarial pattern identified by Vogel in his study of the environmental regulation.)[22] This ideology of cooperation is – we shall see in Section 3 – a legacy of the regulatory reforms of the 1930s. Cooperative regulation does not mean that agencies are the 'captives' of private interests. Capture is characteristic only of smaller, less prestigious institutions: the most notorious case was the Federal Home Loan Bank Board whose officials, it was discovered, regularly attended junkets paid for by the regulated.[23] Nor does cooperation mean that abuses are ignored: on the contrary, the 1980s were marked, as we shall see later, by the highly adversarial enforcement of the law against insider dealing. Cooperative regulation also does not rule out a sharpness in language that can seem shockingly frank to English ears.[24] The ideology of cooperative regulation means, rather, that agencies accept as an important part of their function the obligation to maintain the prosperity of their part of the financial services sector.[25] The commitment to ensure that 'its' industry is healthy gives a regulatory agency an activist, and often strategic, rôle in industrial change.

The regulatory bodies are therefore far more than reactive agents in the process of change. Their standard operating procedures, their commitment to defend and expand agency jurisdiction, and their obligation to foster the health of their parts of the financial services sector, make them key actors in the coalitions formed for and against changes in market practices.

The institutional structure not only shapes the organisational coalitions formed around competing positions, it also helps decide in which arenas policy argument is conducted – and the choice of arena in turn influences the terms in which regulatory arguments are conducted and regulatory innovations accomplished. Debates about the regulation of financial services are, to a striking extent, debates about accounting principles (especially in banking) and debates about legal concepts, like forms of financial contract (especially in securities). The consequence is that two professional groups (accountants and lawyers, in the latter case those organised in the securities bar) play a key role: it is their language, their expertise, their competing professional ideologies and their institutional settings (graduate schools, academic journals) which provide the framework for the discussion of regulatory issues. In other words, financial services regulation has to a striking degree experienced something common to other policy-making spheres: it has been professionalised. It is the domain of occupational groups with specialist qualifications; it is conducted in a language of technical complexity, derived from law and accounting; and the key actors in the regulatory process, on the side of firms and agencies, communicate in common professional networks. This has immense implications for the shape taken by debates about regulatory change. In the 1970s, for example, much of the debate about deregulation in the industry was signalled by the growing attention paid by economists to the financial services industry, and by the importation into regulatory debates of 'economic' concepts like efficiency.[26]

The institutional setting of the American financial services industry amounts to more than 'background' to the financial services revolution. The elaborate American legislative framework has created an institutional world within which the struggle for advantage in markets takes place. The world of regulation is populated by a range of public and semi-public agencies, possessing their own ambitions, procedures, functions and hierarchies. They are major actors, and their behaviour is crucial to regulatory outcomes. Understanding the American financial services revolution demands an appreciation of how and why this structure was created. That is the purpose of Section 3.

3   ORIGINS AND EVOLUTION OF MESO-CORPORATISM

The modern American system of financial regulation is the result of three sets of forces: the historical crises that created the system, the institutional legacy available to those who had to construct regulation in the crises, and the subsequent fate of that legacy. The most important crisis was part of a wider catastrophe that overwhelmed the capitalist world at the end of the 1920s. The onset of catastrophe is conventionally marked by the Wall Street Crash of 1929. The 1920s were a period of innovation and growth in American financial services. The linked activities of banking and securities were drawn closely together; new customers were attracted, especially to the booming stock markets; new financiers pioneered new methods. It was an era when financial ingenuity was matched only by financial dishonesty. Sobel has remarked that if a financial 'rascality index' could be constructed the 1920s would be a peak.[27]

The decade culminated in a frenzy of speculation, a collapse of stock market prices, and a wave of bankruptcies.[28] The wider consequences are well known; the financial collapse was associated with a comprehensive international economic crisis, the rise of mass unemployment and the emergence of the New Deal. Before these events there was indeed already some financial regulation, and it was a product of forces similar to those that shaped the system in the 1930s – crisis and the inherited institutional legacy available at the moment of crisis. Thus, the creation in 1913 of the Federal Reserve System was the delayed result of the great banking crisis of 1907. By the early 1930s there had already developed in financial services a fragmented and incomplete meso-corporatist regulation. In the securities markets the greatest Exchange – New York – operated a system of private government, making 'laws and regulations which bear upon its members as strongly as the laws of the land'.[29] In commercial banking the legislation of 1913 had endowed the United States with a Federal Reserve System in which there was a powerful meso-corporatist bias, allowing private bankers significant control.[30]

The Great Crash, with all that it revealed about the scandalous state of Wall Street, discredited this privileged meso-corporatism. There occurred public attacks on standards in the financial services industry – attacks that culminated in widely publicised Congressional hearings of 1932–34 into the abuses of the period. These hearings created the intellectual climate for the reforms pushed through by Roosevelt's first Administration.[31] The most important measures passed between 1933–35 did the following. The banking and securities markets were divided into two controlled segments. Banks were prohibited from entering some of the most important parts of the securities industry. They were also forbidden to pay interest on some deposits, and regulatory ceilings were imposed on other interest payments. Some of the most scandalous financial instruments used before the Great Crash were prohibited. Banks were obliged to contribute to a deposit insurance scheme and an agency – the Federal Deposit Insurance Corporatism – was established to administer that scheme. The Federal Reserve was reorganised to reduce the power of private bankers in the system. A Securities and Exchange Commission was created to oversee controls administered by designated self-regulatory organisations (principally the existing stock exchanges.)[32]

The New Deal Reforms are often pictured as a growth of Federal control over economic life. But their most striking feature in the financial services sector was not so much increasing Federal intervention – though this happened – as the reorganisation and extension of meso-corporatism. Competition in markets was subjected to extensive regulation by Federal Agencies and self-regulatory bodies. A regulatory world was created populated by a network of public and semi-public bodies, individual firms and professional groups like accountants. This regulatory world functioned largely independently of the competitive arenas of democratic politics. The strength of the bias to meso-corporatism of course varied. It was weakest in commercial banking and strongest in the linked areas of investment banking and securities dealing, where there developed a formally organised system of self-regulatory organisations based on the stock exchanges. But it is the reconstruction of an order where private interests were invested with regulatory privileges – in a word meso-corporatism – that is the most striking unifying feature of the reforms of 1933–35.

The reasons for this are traceable to the historical conditions in which reform took place. They emphasise the point made in Chapter 1 – that systems of regulation are deeply imprinted with the shape of the crisis that gives them birth. The great crisis produced by the Wall Street Crash unified many different forces behind reform: a large body of public opinion and elected representatives, scandalised by the business practices of the speculators; and some in the financial community, who were fearful for the economic stability and political legitimacy of the market order.

The consensus over the need for reform also stretched to agreement that the best solution lay in obliging the financial services sector to regulate itself. The prevailing ideology of business regulation stressed the need for 'flexibility', and the best way to ensure flexibility was to put regulation into the hands of practitioners. Where any authority was in the hands of a public agency it should have maximum freedom from Congressional interference. Senator Maloney's judgement, on securities regulation, was representative:

'Congress has undertaken to provide a mechanism whereby the securities business of the country may deal with all problems of technical regulation, leaving to the Securities and Exchange Commission what it is hoped will be the residual position of policing the submarginal fringe.' William Douglas, perhaps the most influential of the New Deal reformers in financial services, put it in similar terms: self-regulatory organisations 'should be so organised as to be able to take on the job of policing their members so that it would be unnecessary for Government to interfere with that business'.[33]

The existence of an ideology of practitioner-based regulation in the 1930s is far more than a historical curiosity. It lies at the heart of the present crisis of meso-corporatism in financial services. The privileged position of private interests was due to nothing so crude as their 'capture' of individual institutions in the regulatory system; it was the most important principle governing the workings of regulation. At the heart of the New Deal lay a system of business regulation displaying a marked bias to corporatism; and at the heart of the system of business regulation lay the arrangements for the regulation of financial markets.

The bias to corporatism was traceable to four influences. The first was the ideological hegemony of business values in a capitalist society – an unsurprising hegemony in a society based on institutions of private property and economic allocation through markets. There was simply a widely held assumption that regulation should be shared with, and not forced upon, the regulated, when the regulated were major property holders and were major participants in markets. These ideological assumptions were supported by an obvious practical consideration. The cooperation of the owners of property rights in the financial services industry was needed because, as long as the market order prevailed, regulation could not be carried out effectively without the cooperation of those who actually operated the markets.

A second, more immediate, factor was that the institutions charged with regulation needed some obvious resources – skilled personnel, information – to carry out the regulatory task. The regulated industries themselves were the chief suppliers of these resources. To take only the most striking example: in securities, the Securities and Exchange Commission had to build an entirely new system of regulation in 1935. Most of those who knew anything about the complicated task of securities regulation were already in the industry. In such circumstances, to do anything other than rely on the regulated would have made the regulatory task impossible.

A third consideration was more immediate still. Although there was a consensus about the need for a 'bias to corporatism', this still left much

room for argument about the extent and form of the bias. In these debates
the financial community had many advantages. Wall Street still retained
many of the traditional resources of a business elite – money, the best
expertise and lobbying capacity that this money could buy, control over
much of the media, plenty of servants in Congress, and excellent social and
political connections. The defeat of many radical schemes of regulation was
in large part due to this power. In all the main items of regulatory reform in
financial markets the pattern was similar – the lobbying process diminished
democratic controls and increased the bias to meso-corporatism.[34]

Ideological hegemony, the control of expertise, and control over political
resources were aided by a final factor: the historical timing of crisis. Studies
of the regulatory agencies created in the 1960s and 1970s have noted how
far the 'new social regulation' was implemented by a class of regulators
separate from, and often hostile to, the regulated business interests.[35] These
regulators were commonly the product of graduate schools governed by a
'public service' ethic, and were intent on making a career in public service.
In other words, they had an outlook and a set of interests that distinguished
them from the business community. Hardly any of this existed in the 1930s.
A complex structure of regulation had to be created quickly, at a historical
moment when there was very little experienced regulatory talent available.
Within the Federal Government itself there were few such individuals, and
even the sources of raw young talent – the law schools, and the graduate
schools in public administration – were, by modern standards, quite small.
In short, the timing of the crisis reinforced the structural advantages
enjoyed by the bankers and financiers – for the state, in the absence of
a cadre of experienced public servants, had little option but to rely on the
industry to provide the expertise and carry out the tasks.[36]

Regulation through meso-corporatism spread through the financial services sector in the 1930s because it helped the industries in the sector meet
two threats: the threat from excessive economic competition in markets,
whose manic and uncontrolled character had nearly destroyed the market
order after 1929; and the threat of political competition from democratic
institutions. The scandalous and dangerous practices that culminated in
the Wall Street Crash showed what perils accompanied a poorly regulated
market order. William Douglas put it best in speaking of the Agencies
created by the New Deal: the regulatory commissions, he remarked,
were 'the outposts of capitalism; they have been given increasingly large
patrol duties lest capitalism, by its own greed, avarice, or myopia destroy
itself'.[37]

The economic purpose of the reforms in banking and securities was to
restrict competition. It did this by creating a system where regulation

and interest representation were closely linked, and where the regulated enjoyed protection against price competition, against the uncontrolled entry into markets by new firms, and against competition by innovation. The 'corporatist bias' suppressed some of the disturbing forces produced by a market order, and gave a privileged position to the interests and institutions already in place when regulation began.

If the economic purpose of the reforms was to protect financial services from competitive excess in the marketplace, the political function was to provide protection against the 'excesses' of democracy. The early 1930s were years of great danger for Wall Street, when it faced widespread popular hostility and political forces demanding that it be publicly regulated. The crisis thus posed a serious threat to the political autonomy of the financial services sector. The bias to corporatism – embodied in doctrines of practitioner regulation, and in institutions working at a safe distance from democratic arenas – was a defence against that threat.

The regulatory history of the 1930s is a key to understanding the present day financial services revolution because the features developed in the New Deal remain engrained in the regulatory structure. The subsequent history of regulation in the industry might be summarised, at risk of simplification, as the attempt to cope with the stresses set up between the bias to corporatism on the one hand, and the pressures of capitalism and of a democratic state, on the other. As we shall see in Section 4 these tensions became acute from the 1960s, and culminated in radical reform during the 1970s and early 1980s.

The regulatory system in the generation after 1935 was thus shaped by the timing of the great crisis of the 1930s. Nevertheless, important changes of a slow and often barely noticed character took place even before the dramatic developments of the 1970s and 1980s. Three of these are worth noting: the changed scale of markets, the changing political environment of regulation, and the altered internal structure of the regulatory system.

The system created in the 1930s was designed to regulate firms operating in American markets. But as America came to dominate the world economy, American banks and securities firms extended their international operations: in 1960, eight banks already had 124 foreign branches; fifteen years later 126 banks had 762 branches abroad.[38] The point is of special significance because a key object of regulation had been to control competition in markets; the 'internationalisation' of the industry moved many firms, notably the largest and most innovative, beyond the jurisdiction of the American regulatory system.That movement became even more noticeable with the development – as described in Chapter 1 – of the Eurodollar markets. One of the chief influences stimulating the growth of the Euromarkets was the American regulatory structure itself. Eurodollar operations offered banks freedom from many domestic banking restrictions – for instance, those on interest rates, and requirements obliging banks to hold a proportion of deposits in low-yielding 'reserve' assets. The markets received a particular boost from the introduction in 1963 of the Interest Equalisation Tax, a measure designed to inhibit foreign issues of securities in America. The tax reflected the efforts of the central institutions of the American state – Presidency and Treasury – to cope with the emerging weaknesses of a once supreme American economy.[39] The rise of the Euromarkets was thus significant for many reasons: because in size they soon outstripped domestic financial markets; because, freed from national restrictions, they provided regulatory laboratories where firms could experiment with competitive innovations; and above all, because they emphasised how the multinational character of markets was transcending a nationally organised system of meso-corporatism.

The second important long-term change concerned what is best summarised as the political environment of the industry. The kind of state that the financial services industry had to deal with was transformed in the generation after the New Deal. The rise of American political and economic power in the international system meant that regulation – especially financial regulation – became entwined with the American state's role as the manager of the international political and economic system, and as the defender of American interests in the struggles for advantage which took place in the system. After 1945 issues of financial regulation – such as price competition and barriers to market entry – were no longer solely a domestic matter; they were entangled with central questions of international economic diplomacy and with the defence and extension of American influence in the international system. As Odell wrote, of the era before the abandonment of dollar convertibility to gold in 1971: 'The U.S. capacity to defend convertibility and to influence the monetary policy of other states rested on the U.S. military position, the global size of the American market and U.S. bargaining capacity, all relative to those of other states.'[40] Thus even before the financial services revolution truly began, regulation was being shaped by the wider character of the international system.

If the American state's international significance was altering, the same was true domestically. The 'bias to corporatism' was pronounced in the 1930s because of the virtual monopoly of regulatory expertise enjoyed by the markets, and because of the corresponding scarcity of regulatory talent available to the Federal Government. In the succeeding generation the agencies concerned with regulation had varied histories – some marked by efficiency, some not. But it was almost impossible, with the accumulation of regulatory experience, for the balance between the industry and the state not to change. The financial services industries lost their virtual monopoly of regulatory expertise. The professionalisation of regulatory knowledge meant that authoritative knowledge fell into the hands of groups like lawyers, accountants and economists. In some degree these professions were controlled by the financial services sector, which was a major consumer of their services. But the traditions of scholarly independence and free debate in a pluralist democracy meant that this control was incomplete. By the 1960s the graduate schools of universities contained numerous figures – like the accountant Benston and the economist Stigler – who were mounting sustained challenges to the prevailing ideologies of regulation.[41]

The agencies, in turn, were benefiting, from the simple accumulation of knowledge and experience. It was commonly and rightly noted that the institutions created by the New Deal typically enjoyed close relations with regulated industries. One of the most obvious signs was the movement of staff between agencies and firms. This was sometimes referred to as the 'revolving door' principle – implying that there was a two-way exchange between the agencies and the industries. Except at the very highest level (for instance, Commissioners in the SEC) the image was inaccurate. In the case of the two most important agencies – the Federal Reserve and the SEC – the movement was mostly one way, out of the agency into the industry. The reason was simple: anybody who moved the other way took a cut in pay. It was recognised that able young lawyers or economists, especially if they enjoyed no family connections, could move into the best firms by first displaying their ability for a few years in a regulatory agency.[42]

In the generation after the 1930s' crisis, therefore, a subtle but important alteration occurred in the institutional balance of the meso-corporatist system: at the beginning the financial services industries were suppliers of expertise to the agencies; over the next generation the agencies became much less dependent, until they were themselves a source of talent for firms. This changing balance was accompanied by a growth in the prestige and self-confidence of the agencies. The most striking case is the Securities and Exchange Commission. The infant of the 1930s soon acquired a reputation as one of the most successful of the New Deal institutions, and became the single most important repository of information about the securities industry. Something of this alteration is suggested by the landmark *Special study* conducted by an SEC team in the early 1960s. It was the most exhaustive examination of the industry carried out till that time (or since). Its sharply critical analysis of the system of regulation, – especially of the performance of the stock exchanges as self-regulatory organisations – foreshadowed many of the policy debates and reforms of the 1970s, and indicated the confidence with which a prestigious regulatory agency could now analyse the industry, in contrast to the deference shown practitioners in the 1930s.[43] The changing institutional balance was not unique to financial services. It was part of a general shift identified by Lowi. In the 1930s, he remarks, the state recognised private associations out of weakness: 'it was forced to share its sovereignty in return for support.' By the 1960s, in contrast, the arrangements were 'voluntarily pursued as the highest expression of their ideology'.[44]

In the intervening decades after the crisis of the 1930s the parts of the American state involved in the regulation of the financial services became, to adapt Krasner's language, 'stronger' relative to the interests they were regulating.[45] They developed independent expertise, became suppliers of specialised personnel to the industry and, especially in the case of the SEC and the Federal Reserve, acquired considerable public prestige.

Meanwhile the 'practitioners' themselves had altered. This was the third long-term change that came over the regulatory system in the decades after the New Deal reforms. 'Practitioner based regulation' in the 1930s meant just that – regulation by individuals most of whose time was devoted to their normal business life. Over the decades there grew up a separate group of regulators. In the biggest banks and brokerage houses the regulatory function – which meant both applying internal rules, and negotiating with external bodies – emerged as a separate and specialised corporate role, usually performed by appropriately qualified lawyers and accountants. Self-regulation, the key part of meso-corporatism, was being taken out of the hands of practical businessmen and placed under control of professionals like lawyers. As early as 1963 the SEC observed the change in its Special Study. It remarked of self-regulation that

> a constantly changing group of part-time volunteers whose self-regulatory activity must be performed at the expense of their business pursuits could not, unaided, hope to supply the unified and continuous organisation . . . necessary to accomplish the job . . . this has inevitably led to compromise with the ideal of self-regulation by industry members – and the special advantages associated with it – in the direction of increasing reliance on full-time staff.[46]

This growing domination of regulation by professionals is central to the story of the crisis of meso-corporatism. In a pluralist democracy ideological mystification is limited by the need to justify regulatory arrangements in the language of rational policy discourse. The claim that financial regulation was something mysterious and delicate that only practitioners could do had, by the 1960s, to be sustained in a very different institutional world from that prevailing in the 1930s. It was now a world where the professional networks of economists, lawyers and accountants allowed numerous informed and technically qualified individuals to intervene in regulatory debates. This was to prove an important factor in the regulatory upheavals of the 1970s and 1980s – to which we now turn.

4   STRUCTURAL CHANGE AND THE CRISIS OF MESO-CORPORATISM

We already know, from Chapter 1, something of the general characteristics of the financial services revolution. But to understand how that revolution caused a regulatory crisis in the United States we need to find out more about the way it was experienced there. The essence of that experience can be summarised as follows. The most important purpose of the system of regulation created in the 1930s was to restrain competition. It did this by giving to private interests economic privileges and regulatory duties. The economic and political balance of the system was upset because in the 1960s and 1970s new opportunities became available to pursue the struggle for competitive advantage in markets. New competitive opportunities created new interests, and changed the nature of established interests. Meso-corporatism was pitched into a crisis because the corporatist system proved unable either to suppress or to incorporate the new interests created by competitive struggle. Reforms introduced in the mid-1970s in securities regulation partly resolved the crisis, at the expense of creating a more hierarchical and state-controlled system. But the wider structural changes resulting from the reforms of the mid-1970s have intensified competitive struggles. They are culminating in an attack on the last great barrier to economic competition erected in the 1930s, the Glass-Steagall Act separating investment from commercial banking.

The struggle to adapt to structural change is part of the story of the financial revolution. But there is also another part. The age of financial change has also been an age of financial scandal, in the United States and elsewhere. Scandal, we shall see in Section 5, was a key source of regulatory change in America in the 1980s. But it was also a crucial factor in causing the reforms of the 1970s. The central part played by scandal is intimately connected to the ideology of meso-corporatism. Like all ideologies, part of its function was to mystify – in this case to represent financial regulation as a task so delicate and complex that it could only be carried out in a flexible and effective way by the regulated themselves. By the 1960s, however, this ideology had to survive in an environment where mystification was immensely difficult. There were numerous social agents ready to ask sceptical questions about the true effectiveness of flexible, practitioner-based regulation. Some of these agents were inside the regulatory system itself – something we noticed in the last section. But there were also wider forces at work. Meso-corporatism in financial services had to demonstrate its regulatory competence in a competitive political system and in a culture often sceptical – especially in the 1960s and early 1970s – of business honesty and competence.[47] The task was further complicated because the system was indeed often inefficient and dishonest. Meso-corporatist institutions were thus vulnerable to scandals and crisis. These affairs – like the 'back office' crisis that we examine later – were turning points in the arguments about regulatory change, because they helped discredit the defenders of the established order. 'Scandal and crisis' is thus an important theme because it helps explain why regulatory change happened, and because it explains why the drift of regulatory reform has been towards greater state control over the institutions of meso-corporatism. It is also significant because it anticipates a theme which will be important when we turn to Britain and Japan. Meso-corporatism in the American system is particularly vulnerable, because mechanisms of ideological demystification are especially potent in an open and democratic society. In the United Kingdom and Japan hierarchies, deference and secrecy are much stronger; but even in those nations, we shall see, scandal has been an important agent of regulatory change.

The immediate causes of intensified competitive struggles have been well documented in the economic literature on the financial services revolution.[48] They can for convenience be summarised under the linked headings of internationalisation and technological innovation. Banking and securities markets were particularly influenced by internationalisation. A number of forces drew the biggest American firms into international markets. Many of the most important industrial customers of banks expanded to a multinational scale, and financial services firms were obliged to follow them abroad. Likewise, firms had to adapt to the rise of international capital markets like the Eurodollar market. Once abroad, outside their own national regulatory jurisdictions, they naturally soon learnt to extend competitive struggles into areas prohibited by domestic regulation.

Although technological change was closely connected to this internationalisation of markets, technology has also long had an independent bearing on the financial services industry. In the nineteenth century, for instance, the invention of the telegraph, the telephone and the ticker tape machine all deeply affected the scale and organisation of financial markets.[49] In the post-war years improved international communication, especially with the advent of satellites, encouraged financial trading on an international scale.

Domestically, the development of sophisticated telecommunications systems, harnessed to computing power, changed the social organisation of markets and the conditions under which trading took place. In securities it allowed the creation of sophisticated networks that dispensed with a traditional stock exchange 'floor'. In commercial banking it offered numerous possibilities for circumventing regulatory barriers.[50]

The concepts of internationalisation and technological change provide powerful explanations for the crisis of meso-corporatism in the American financial services industry, but in one respect they are subtly misleading. They convey the idea that the political creations of meso-corporatism were being challenged by the impersonal forces of technology and the impersonal laws of markets. But those forces were themselves shaped by particular historical circumstances. 'Internationalisation' – to take the most obvious example – did not consist in the symmetrical integration of financial centres world wide. It meant the growing Americanisation of the financial services sector worldwide: it was the American dollar that was the dominant currency of world exchange, and the American financial services firms who led in the process of international expansion. This state of affairs obviously reflected the single most striking feature of the world after 1945: the extent to which the international system was dominated by American power.[51] Obvious though the point is, it nevertheless merits emphasis because, as we shall see, the challenges to that power proved critical to the world financial services revolution in the 1980s. The central role of technological innovation likewise reflected the position of the United States at the top of the international hierarchy. The most important technology-induced innovations have used the linked technologies of computers and (satellite assisted) telecommunications – sectors where, for most of the period, the United States was the world leader.[52]

Internationalisation and technological innovation corroded the two economic pillars of meso-corporatism: the restrictions on price competition and the legal barriers segregating markets. The most important restrictive practices in banking – limits to price competition in the form of interest rate restrictions, and barriers to market entry like those in the legislation against the formation of inter-state branch networks – proved easy victims. Limits to price competition could be circumvented by moving business abroad to Euromarkets. Domestically, banks used a combination of technology and legal inventiveness to create accounts that paid interest linked to returns on deposits in wholesale money markets, but having no other characteristics of a retail bank account.[53] Technology was likewise used to leap barriers to entry to different geographical markets: nationwide networks of automated teller machines, offering the payment and withdrawal services of a bank branch, allowed the creation, despite legislative prohibitions, of cross-state banking networks.[54] These offensive measures provoked counter offensive and defensive responses from competitors. Banks, securities firms and insurance companies all became involved in offensive and defensive attacks on each others markets. This undermined one of the key principles of meso-corporatism, the organisation of interests into separate markets enjoying privileged protection from competition.

The developments described here should not be seen as a clear battle between firms in markets on the one hand, and regulators on the other. The essential feature of the American regulatory system lay (indeed still lies) in its fusion of the public and private spheres, and in the creation of networks linking interests across the conventional public/private divide. Most institutions, whether firms or agencies, were subject to contradictory pressures. The positions they adopted were determined by the internal coalition that happened to be in the ascendant in the particular institution. If no winning coalition existed, the institution simply became immobile: the SEC was, we shall shortly see, hopelessly split in the early 1970s over key issues of regulatory change. Even individual firms were in contradictory positions.[55] The biggest securities firms, for instance, loyally defended the separation of investment from commercial banking in attempts to keep commercial banks out of the securities business; at the same time they hungrily eyed, and sometimes surreptitiously feasted upon, commercial banking markets. Some of the most enthusiastic destroyers of the regulatory structure were actually in the regulatory agencies. The office of Comptroller of the Currency, an arm of the Treasury responsible for implementing the highly restrictive banking regulations of that era, was one of the main sources of regulatory innovations designed to circumvent restrictions on competition.[56]

The regulatory changes are thus much more than a matter of inventive markets beating restrictive regulators. Nor do they just amount to the piecemeal erosion of meso-corporatism through economic change. That is indeed part of the story, but not the most important part. The greatest change came at a single revolutionary moment in 1975, when there took place a simultaneous reorganisation of economic practices and a significant reallocation of authority within the meso-corporatist structure. The two events were the decision to phase out fixed minimum commissions for brokerage transactions on the New York Stock Exchange; and the passage by Congress of the Securities Acts Amendments. The first of these was important even when viewed against the background of the securities industry, because the decision mandated price competition on what was then the world's largest stock exchange. But the significance of the reform was wider still: by unfreezing the competitive structure on the Exchange it began an era of rapid change in Wall Street and, as an extension, throughout the financial system.[57] The events in 1975 have some claim to be the decisive moment in the American financial services revolution; and, because the United States has been a world leader, they might without exaggeration be described as a critical moment in the world financial services revolution.

The Securities Amendments Acts also transformed regulation, but in a different way. The legislation did three things: it increased the power of the SEC over self-regulatory organisations; increased the authority of SROs over their members; and laid down more detailed guidelines for the behaviour of institutions in the system. In short, in 1975 meso-corporatism was subjected to greater codification, institutionalisation and juridification.[58]

Many puzzles surround these events. The most elementary concerns how it was ever possible to mobilise a legislative majority in Congress. At a deeper level, there exists the mystery of explaining how a wider reforming coalition was created, when the major institutional actors were internally fragmented by contradictory interests and pressures. Finally, there is the mystery of the apparent contradictions in the substance of the changes: the end of minimum commissions fitted an obvious pattern of 'deregulation'; but this decision was imposed on private interests in the New York Stock Exchange by the Securities and Exchange Commission, while the legislation itself actually subjected meso-corporatism to more regulation.

The reconstruction of these events shows, unsurprisingly, that the outcomes were influenced by contingent events – 'incidents' of the particular time, individual scandals. But these contingencies were given meaning because by the end of the 1960s the system of meso-corporatism originally created in the 1930s had become politically vulnerable. The interests to whom it gave a specially privileged position had lost much of their significance in the markets, and the new interests were not incorporated, in part because of resistance by those given privileges in the original system. Beyond the markets, institutional and cultural changes were demystifying the ideology of self-regulation. By the late 1960s the system was ripe for assault from excluded interests, and was ripe also for attacks on the efficacy of self-regulation, the institutional core of meso-corporatism. These attacks indeed happened – and their outcome was the reforms of the mid-1970s.

The crux of the economic arguments concerned the position of the New York Stock Exchange, and its system of minimum commissions on bargains. It might at first glance seem unlikely that such a particular issue as the abolition of minimum brokerage commissions on a single exchange would be of significance; but in fact it held the key to structural change in the securities industry. The New York Exchange is, and has been historically, by far the most important in the securities industry: for instance, in the year reforms were finally made, 1975, it accounted for 80 per cent of the volume, and 85 per cent of the dollar value, of the business of all American exchanges.[59] The ban on price competition – which was what the system of minimum commissions amounted to – also put a stop to the structural change that is an inevitable outcome of competitive struggles.

The system of minimum commissions was the historical cornerstone of the New York Stock Exchange in a quite exact sense, because it was the Buttonwood Tree Agreement of 1792 (fixing an agreed commission rate) which is generally agreed to mark the foundation of the Exchange.[60] By the 1960s minimum commissions conferred powerful advantages on member firms. The size of the Exchange meant that it dominated trading in most prestigious stocks in the American economy. Dealings in listed stock could in turn only be conducted through members, and a condition of membership of the Exchange was willingness to charge a minimum commission on bargains transacted.

The case of the New York Stock Exchange illustrates to perfection the kind of tensions contained in the system of meso-corporatism. The privileged position of the Exchange originated in the regulatory structure created in the 1930s, and in the ideologies of practitioner-based regulation that governed the workings of that structure. In other words, we see here how the dominant position of business interests ensured the 'bias to meso-corporatism', allowing private interests to control the regulation of markets. But what would happen when these private interests were guilty of abuses, or were challenged by new interests created through competitive struggles? The prevailing ideology of regulation meant that the one agency with power to intervene, the Securities and Exchange Commission, was almost always unwilling to do so. In its first thirty years of life the Commission only twice used its powers to impose rules on exchanges and only once suspended the regulatory licence of an exchange.[61] Even the revelation at the end of the 1950s that the American Stock Exchange was run by a corrupt oligarchy failed to prompt use of the powers of suspension.[62] In 1972 a Senate sub-committee summed up the history of meso-corporatist regulation as follows: 'a substantial part of the formation of regulatory policy for the securities industry is carried out by means of private consultation between the (SEC) or its staff and one or more of the self-regulatory agencies.'[63] The theory and reality of self-regulation thus meant private bargaining, and a veto over change by those put into a privileged position by the system. The practical result was that, even when the campaign against price fixing reached a crescendo in the early 1970s, the SEC was reluctant to use its powers against the Exchange.

The campaign against minimum commissions illustrates to perfection the problem of operating meso-corporatism in market economies, distinguished as they are by struggles for competitive advantage and by constant structural change. The first challenges came between 1963 and 1966, from ambitious entrepreneurs outside the privileged circle of NYSE membership who tried to undercut the Exchange's price cartel by offering a cut-price brokerage service on some NYSE listed stock. The Exchange reacted by prohibiting its members from doing business with the firms. The response of the excluded showed one of the fatal weaknesses of meso-corporatism in a pluralist democracy, offering as it does many alternative arenas of political struggle. The firms discriminated against by NYSE did what any aggrieved American does automatically: they sued in the courts.[64]

One of the obvious features of a pluralist society is that it contains not only a plurality of political arenas, but also a plurality of competing ideologies. The ideology of self-regulation by practitioners dominated the financial services sector. In the courts, however, other powerful ideologies were at work. One of the most important was – indeed still is – the ideology of anti-trust, a structure of ideas embodied in anti-trust law, dominant in many legal institutions and powerful in the education of a large section of the legal profession. When the NYSE was taken into the courts in the 1960s and required to justify its system of minimum commissions, the ideology supporting meso-corporatism encountered the competing ideology of anti-trust. Although none of the particular challenges to the NYSE succeeded, the text of the judgements showed that there existed in the mind of the courts grave doubts about how far price fixing as practised by the Exchange was compatible with anti-trust law.[65]

Ideologies acquire their power in part from the extent to which they penetrate major social institutions. Meso-corporatist ideology held sway on much of Wall Street and – though with a decreasing hold – in the SEC. Anti-trust ideologies had penetrated great legal institutions – including the Antitrust Division of the Federal Government's own Justice Department. As we saw in Section 2, agencies in the federal system are constantly jockeying to enter each other's jurisdictional domains. In 1968 the Justice Department put the full weight of its institutional prestige, and of anti-trust ideology, behind a public critique of the anti-competitive character of the system of minimum commissions – a critique which it was to repeat and elaborate in and out of Congress for many years.[66] The Department was also able to mobilise the intellectual resources of the economics profession to support the challenge to meso-corporatist ideology. The development of economics as a prestigious discipline with members entrenched in government, research institutes, and universities has been highly damaging to ideologies of practitioner-based, business regulation. It has created intellectually prestigious accounts of how the market economy works that offer an alternative, and a challenge, to the mystifications of self-regulation. One of the most striking features of the debate ignited by the Justice Department was the breadth of opposition to the NYSE among economists: from Chicago-style efficient market theorists, to leading Keynesians like Samuelson, they supported the Justice Department's critique.[67] The example of economists only illustrates in a particular way the embattled character of meso-corporatism in a pluralist democracy.

The mobilisation of an ideology of anti-trust was now given added impetus by yet another consequence of structural change. In the 1950s and 1960s the nature of stock ownership in America changed radically: the proportion of stocks owned by private investors declined; financial institutions became major shareholders of securities. In 1955, institutions owned an estimated 15 per cent by value of stock on the New York Exchange; in 1975 the figure had risen to 35 per cent.[68] The constant change so characteristic of a developed market economy had yet again created a new interest demanding representation. That interest was damaged by the system of minimum commissions: the institutions traded large blocks of shares, but were offered no discount for volume. On the brokers' side the arrangement was hugely profitable: the work in broking 100 000 shares was not significantly greater than the work in broking 1000, but the commission was a hundred times larger. The institutions first tried to buy their way into the circle of privilege, attempting to persuade the NYSE to change its rules to allow them to purchase membership. When this was resisted they put their considerable resources behind the anti-trust critique of minimum commissions.

It will be instructive if we now pause for a moment to consider the condition of meso-corporatism at the moment in 1968 when the Justice Department first fired its salvo against the NYSE. In the crisis created after the Wall Street Crash business interests managed, amazingly, to retain the ideological high ground. Regulatory reform was guided by the almost universal assumption that the regulated interest knew best how to conduct the details of regulation. The law was, to use Douglas's vivid metaphor, 'a shotgun behind the door'[69] – only taken up to pick off the odd miscreant, and perhaps to fire the occasional warning volley over the heads of the business community. Secular changes inseparable from the capitalist and democratic character of the United States changed the environment in which this ideology tried to function. Sources of expertise about regulation developed that were distinct from, and often independent of, private interests: in the Federal agencies, in academic institutions and in the courts.

Competitive struggle and structural change created new interests to challenge those in a position of privilege. The alternative ideologies always available in a pluralist democracy meant that intellectually coherent challenges could indeed be fashioned. An intellectually coherent defence of meso-corporatism in general, and of the particular arrangements in the securities industry, was of course also possible; but it had to be, precisely, intellectually coherent. Meso-corporatist ideology no longer commanded the high ground. It was not possibly simply to assume that private interests know best how to practise regulation; the defenders of the old order now had to descend into arenas like the courts and Congress to demonstrate that practitioner based self-regulation produced honest and efficient business practices. They had to demonstrate this against the challenge of alternative ideologies, like anti-trust, that were now supported by powerful interests. Those interests would not hesitate to seize on any examples of dishonesty and efficiency. We can see with the benefit of hindsight that the old order was in a perilous state, pregnant with the risk of crisis and scandal.

By 1967 this crisis was, indeed, already upon meso-corporatism, though its full significance had yet to be recognised. It was the 'back office' crisis on the New York Stock Exchange which began in that year. The immediate cause lay in the unceasing competitive struggles of a market economy. The Exchange witnessed one of the periodic speculative manias that punctuate the history of all financial markets. In the struggle to attract the flood of customers the 'back office organisation' of many firms – the section processing the deals transacted for customers – collapsed in chaos. There were serious breaches of trading rules and substantial losses by investors. The Exchange's own Compensation Fund proved quite insufficient (indeed, it was forced to raid its Building Fund to help compensate for losses). In 1969–70, 160-member firms went out of business.[70] Congress was obliged to establish a Securities Investor Protection Corporation to provide insurance against future failure.

The back office crisis was the single most direct cause of the 1975 legislation that codified, institutionalised and juridified the system of meso-corporatism. The SEC's own study of the affair, a devastating catalogue of regulatory incompetence, was presented to Congress in late 1971. Its recommendations for reform were embodied in statute over the next four years. The crisis also contributed to the Commission's 1973 ruling that the NYSE must phase out its arrangements for fixing minimum commissions from 1975.[71] The chaos and failures on Wall Street were a great blow to the claim that self-regulation used the unique skill of expert practitioners. With the appearance in 1971 of the SEC's study of the affair, the debate about the whole character of the self-regulatory system moved into Congress. In 1971–72 Committees of both Houses conducted detailed hearings and investigations on the system of financial regulation. They were more detailed even than those held in the crisis of the early 1930s. These hearings provided a golden opportunity for the conflicting interests created by structural change to argue in public, and for the ideologists of anti-trust to refashion their attacks.[72] Even before the hearings began, the New York Stock Exchange started to offer concessions – for instance, price discounts on the large volume trades done by the big institutions.[73] The concession proved worthless, merely emphasising the weakened position of meso-corporatist ideology. Once that ideology had lost the high ground of unthinking, widespread acceptance, it had to be sufficiently intellectually coherent to meet the challenge of alternative ideologies, like anti-trust, in arenas where it would be tested, like the courts. But there was no coherence in a position that offered competition and price discounts to big, rich institutional investors while denying them to small private investors.

The final sign that the ideological foundations of the old order were collapsing came with the evidence of divisions inside the Securities and Exchange Commission. A complex organisation like the SEC is obviously influenced by the pluralist society in which it operates. The highly critical report on the back office crisis showed that there were plenty of people inside the organisation unimpressed by traditional regulatory ideologies. The Commission's failure to move against the NYSE in the 1960s is probably explicable by the continuing domination of ideologies of practitioner-based regulation; the failure to move decisively in the early 1970s was more the result of organisational deadlock between the supporters and opponents of change. The exact timing of the breaking of the deadlock was influenced by SEC involvement in the adjacent scandal of Watergate. The corporate corruption that was part of Watergate implicated the SEC Chairman, Bradford Cooke, a Nixon appointment. The discrediting of Nixon and his appointees led to the appointment as Commissioners of several independent and respected members of the securities bar who decisively tipped the balance of opinion in favour of reform.[74]

The back office crisis was a direct cause of the 1975 Securities Amendments Acts, and a powerful contributor to the SEC – mandated unfixing of commission rates in the same year. But it was also significant in a more diffuse way: it demonstrated the vulnerability of meso-corporatism to scandal and crisis, and anticipated two decades of critical and scandalous episodes. This was not because behaviour in markets became more reprehensible. It was because, having lost ideological hegemony, meso-corporatist regulation was now subject to intense critical scrutiny. One pattern in financial regulation during the 1970s and 1980s can be interpreted as the liberalisation of market practices – a widely-known process involving the removal of barriers to price competition and market entry. But the other, contradictory, pattern is the growing codification, institutionalistion and juridification of the system of regulation, in the effort either to prevent scandals and crisis, or to manage the consequences when they have happened.

The landmark legislation of 1975 was just such an episode in crisis management. Likewise, after scandals and failures in the important municipal securities markets, regulation there was overhauled to strengthen the SEC's regulatory role.[75] In 1974 the futures markets, traditionally subject to only the lightest public control, were reorganised under a Federal Agency (Commodity Futures Trading Commission) and a set of self-regulatory organisations.[76] The International Banking Act of 1978 extended federal powers over foreign bank branches in America. The Depository Institutions Deregulation and Monetary Control Act (1980) indeed mandated the end of administered ceilings on interest rates – but it also made membership of the Federal Reserve System for the first time obligatory for a wide range of deposit-taking institutions.[77] Indeed, one of the persistent themes of regulation was the search for a 'super-regulator' – a supreme institution capable of uniting and controlling the present dispersed regulatory structure.[78]

Scandal, and the fear of scandal, thus became a decisive influence on financial regulation. This was nowhere more obvious than in the most widely publicised area of financial regulation in recent years – the control of insider trading, to which we next turn.

5   INSIDER TRADING AND MESO-CORPORATISM

'Insider trading' became in the 1980s the single best known aspect of the American financial markets. Securities markets were invested by novelists, film directors and playwrights with a seedy glamour commonly held to typify the 'yuppie' culture of the decade. The front pages of the newspapers were filled with a continuous series of scandals. Some of these concerned the press itself: a reporter on the *Wall Street Journal* was convicted of using pre-publication information for profitable speculation. Others concerned senior political figures, like Paul Thayer, a leading official in President Reagan's first Administration, who in 1985 pleaded guilty to feeding inside information to friends for purposes of profitable speculation.[79]

Still more scandals implicated – and, as I write, continue to implicate – major firms and respected figures in the financial markets. In 1986 Ivan Boesky became the most famous disgraced financier since Richard Whitney (the head of the New York Stock Exchange who went to Sing Sing in 1938). Mr Boesky disgorged over $100 million of a fortune acquired by insider trading; was subsequently jailed for the modest period of two years; and as part of his plea bargaining named numerous respected figures on Wall Street as accomplices.[80] In February 1987 police, accompanied by television cameras, raided a number of elite Wall Street investment houses and led away senior figures in handcuffs. In short, the 'war' against insider trading has taken on the typical characteristics of American enforcement – it is highly public, adversarial and is sweeping a tide of scandal into the upper reaches of American political and economic elites.[81]

It was widely concluded that these scandals were not isolated instances of human venality, but reflected more enduring changes in the culture of the financial services sector. The most influential account held, indeed, that there was a close connection between the problem of insider trading and the changes discussed in Section 4 of this chapter; in other words that the intensification of competition, coupled with changes in the scale of business and in the ownership structure, had weakened moral codes and undermined honesty.[82]

We shall see there is indeed a good deal in the notion that the insider trading scandals and the wider changes in the industry are connected – but the connection is more complex than the one usually made. Insider trading did become more lucrative in the 1970s and 1980s, because a booming stock market, coupled with waves of hotly-contested take overs, meant that the rewards of anticipating price changes using advance information were enormous. Inside knowledge of impending takeovers was the foundation of Mr Boesky's enormous fortune. Yet while the rewards of insider trading are great it is, we shall see, almost certainly the case that the practice itself has become less common. Insider dealing became a widely recognised regulatory problem at the very moment of its decline. There is indeed a connection with the purge against insider dealing and the wider regulatory changes sketched earlier; but the connection is not that the new regulatory order unleashed a novel flood of criminal or unethical practices as a result of 'deregulation' (although it is probably the case that old vices became newly rewarding). 'Deregulation', we have seen, did not happen; on the contrary, the regulatory order became more codified, formally organised and juridified. The 'war on insider trading' is actually part of that development – or, to be more exact, is part of the way scandal and regulatory change are connected. It is, in short, another episode in the demystification of the original ideology that legitimised the system created in the 1930s.

It is sensible to begin with a description of both the nature of the activity and its regulatory history. Insider trading can be defined as the practice of dealing for gain using non-public information acquired through privileged access to the details of an enterprise. We can see immediately that it is a lawyer's paradise: the uncertain meanings of 'non-public' and 'privileged access' make it so. The law was, historically, largely indifferent to the practice. In Hazen's words, 'early common law cases held that in a faceless market insiders had no duty to refrain from trading in their corporation's stock when armed with material inside information'.[83] The securities legislation of 1933 and 1934 did not deal with the practice (although the anti-fraud provisions of the law were subsequently used by the SEC as the basis for its regulatory interventions).[84]

This neglect signified not the absence of insider trading, but indifference to its existence. The great boom of the 1920s was marked by the most extreme abuses designed to rig markets for the benefit of speculators. Yet one of the most successful speculators of the age Joseph Kennedy – a man whose business practices make Ivan Boesky's seem merely venial – was appointed Chairman of the new Securities and Exchange Commission.[85]

Although the SEC first produced a regulation on the subject in 1941, and the initial important court judgment came in 1947, it was not until the late 1970s that the full flood of cases began.[86] This history is due to two linked considerations: the objective difficulties of regulating insider trading; and the ideology that shaped the meso-corporatist system created in the 1930s. The battle against insider trading has been called an 'unwinnable' war.[87] Regulators face acute problems of surveillance and detection. Shapiro's study of fraud detection in the industry shows that even comparatively sophisticated systems often fail to pick up forbidden practices. Surveillance systems rely on the possibility of monitoring active trading, since they work by detecting 'unusual ' trading patterns – mostly unexpected surges of buying at key periods, like that before an announced take-over bid.[88] Yet the possession of privileged information can be just as certainly used profitably to abstain from trade – as when an individual refrains from buying in the knowledge that an impending announcement will depress prices. Even the convictions of Boesky and of his associates relied heavily on old fashioned informing by accused financiers anxious to bargain with their prosecutors, rather than on high technology.

The practical difficulties of detection are made more acute by the problem of defining the nature of insider dealing itself. Opposition to insider trading is rooted in ideas of 'fairness', and in particular in the notion that there should be what practitioners sometimes call a 'level playing field'. This is allied to conceptions of 'fiduciary obligation' – in other words to the idea that those who, by virtue of a position of trust, thereby obtain privileged information should not abuse that trust by using it to trade profitably. The identification of those who should owe such an obligation has, however, proved extraordinarily difficult. There have been extensive arguments over what counts as a position of trust, and for good reason. If those owing a 'fiduciary duty' are restricted in number – for instance, to the directors and senior managers of an enterprise – then detection is in principle possible by obliging fiduciaries to register and disclose all trades made. In the 1970s and 1980s, however, the definition of an insider widened well beyond the range of those directly involved with a business: among the land mark cases, for instance, were those of a football coach alleged to have abused privilege because he traded on the basis of information overheard at a match; a printer who, employed to produce prospectuses for take-over bids, used the advance information thus gained to trade in advance of the publication of the offer; and a number of reporters who used their access to pre-publication information to buy stock in firms whose shares were recommended in the investment columns of their publications.[89]

In brief, insider trading is a practice difficult to detect without a considerable surveillance and enforcement capacity; and impossible to prosecute without an elaborate framework of jurisprudence. The meso-corporatist ideology of practitioner-based regulation dominant from the 1930s was designed precisely to keep these features out of financial life. It is thus no surprise that insider dealing was a matter of indifference in the 1930s. But we know that this ideology began to lose its hegemonic status in the 1960s, and underwent a crisis in the 1970s. We should therefore expect from the 1960s the beginnings of a regulatory campaign in the SEC and in the courts, and we would predict an intensified campaign from the late 1970s. This is precisely what happened.

The first significant modern SEC regulatory intervention dates from 1961. A series of later court judgements in the decade after 1968, usually on SEC initiative, then widened the definition of insider trading, and criminalised the activity. The stream of cases quickened with time: of all insider trading cases brought by the SEC between 1949 and 1983, for instance, over a fifth were filed in the first three years of the 1980s.[90] In 1984 Congress passed the Insider Trading Sanctions Act. This law greatly increased the level of civil damages which could be sought against those convicted of insider dealing. Even more significant, it criminalised whole new markets. For the first time, insider trading in futures and in options was explicitly prohibited.[91] This was the background to the events of 1986 and after – the hunting down of Boesky, the arrests on Wall Street and, as we shall see in later chapters, the development of an international campaign against insider dealing.

The ferocious campaign against insider trading in the 1980s is in many ways an astonishing development. The Reagan administration was acknowledged to be close to Wall Street. The practice itself is almost impossible to define and very difficult to detect. Ideologies of deregulation, a significant part of Reaganism, would have suggested abstention. Indeed economists of a liberal persuasion, like Manne and Stigler, have argued that prohibition is futile and harmful: insider dealing, according to this view, is simply one of the ways information can be transmitted through markets, and one of the means by which the enterprises can reward their managers.[92] Yet despite an Administration sympathetic to Wall Street, an ideology of 'deregulation' that would suggest abstention, and powerful intellectual support from the newly fashionable liberal economists, the 1980s were marked by a purge against the practice. The sceptical reader, aware of suspicions that figures like Mr Boesky actually escaped with comparatively light punishment, might quarrel with this image of a purge. Sceptics can point to the probability that much insider dealing still goes undetected, that the regulatory resources devoted to surveillance and pursuit are quite inadequate, and that the resources of the SEC have failed to match the growth of the markets. There is indeed substance to these critical observations. As in most 'white collar crime', detection, prosecution and conviction are limited by powerful cultural forces. In the eyes of some, insider trading, if it is a crime, is a crime without a victim. Yet the magnitude of historical change should not be minimised. Insider dealing is not prosecuted with the fullest vigour; but the change in assumptions on the part of regulators, judges, firms and legislators in recent decades is remarkable. Ivan Boesky's punishment may not have been commensurate with his activities; but equally his disgrace was a world away from the treatment given to an earlier successful manipulator, Joseph Kennedy, who was rewarded with the Chairmanship of the SEC and an Ambassadorship. Reagan was tougher on Wall Street than was Roosevelt.

The nature and the timing of the Reaganite attack on insider dealing are partly explicable by some general characteristics of American regulation, and partly by the changed nature of meso-corporatism in financial services. Business regulation in America has been described as 'adversarial' by Vogel. Although much regulation in financial services is, on the contrary, highly cooperative, there is no doubt that the drive against insider dealing has been influenced by adversarial notions and an enforcement mentality. It is difficult to imagine prominent City figures in London being arrested in their offices and led away in hand cuffs to spend a night in the cells on suspicion of insider dealing, as occurred in New York in 1987. In the 1980s some ambitious attorneys undoubtedly felt that there was a career advancement to be had from the public pursuit of those suspected of insider dealing.

Yet the tradition of adversarial regulation was always present. It therefore cannot be used to answer the key questions: why did the purge of insider dealing originate in the 1960s and reach a peak in the late 1980s? The reasons for this have to do with the terms of the meso-corporatist 'contract' in the 1930s, the resurgence of the struggle for comparative advantage in the markets, and wider changes in the American political system in the 1960s and 1970s.

We have seen that meso-corporatism was originally supported by an ideology that protected business privilege. This ideology pictured regulation as an activity suited only to practitioners capable of responding 'flexibly' to changing market conditions. The ideology had, however, lost its hegemonic status by the late 1960s. Business control over the regulatory process could no longer be justified on the grounds that property holders, merely by virtue of their legal position, had the right to organise markets as they wished. The justification of business privilege shifted from the absolute rights of private property to a more contingent argument – that business could do the job of regulation better than any other agency. This left meso-corporatism vulnerable to any crisis or scandal, since such occurrences could be used to show the practical ineffectiveness of regulation. In the United States, a liberal society with a competitive polity, there existed numerous potential critics – in the press, in Congress, in the regulatory agencies – ready to ask awkward questions about the efficacy of existing arrangements whenever some failure took place. For about three decades after 1935, this vulnerability was contained because the community concerned with regulating financial markets was small, and its language esoteric. It attracted little attention from the wider political system. The ferocious struggles for comparative advantage since then have, as we saw in Section 4, changed all that. The politicisation of the industry transformed the treatment of issues which for a generation had been talked about only in the esoteric language of the securities bar and the accounting profession. This aroused the interest of journalists and Congressmen – hence the incentive to ambitious young regulators to pursue figures like Boesky.

The regulatory system has thus become vulnerable to scandal and crisis. We saw earlier how this worked in the case of the back office crisis in the late 1960s. Insider dealing has some obvious features that make it an even more suitable object for scandal: it has been widespread; it offends many deeply-held popular notions about what constitutes fairness in a business exchange; and it brings great, effortless rewards to its practitioners. Of course the same could be said about numerous other trading practices in financial markets. The particular focus on insider dealing is connected to the issue attention process among those, like journalists and politicians, who deal in 'abuses'. Insider trading, if we view it as fraud is, for all its legal complexities, in essence a fraud which is simple to grasp and therefore easy to represent and dramatise in policy arguments about abuses. This helps explain why it has been the single most important recent source of scandal in American financial markets – and, to anticipate, why the concern with this scandal has been so successfully 'exported' to other countries, like the United Kingdom and Japan. (It also explains the success of popular dramatisations in films and other fictional forms.)

The purge against insider dealing is thus part of the continuing crisis of meso-corporastism, a crisis whose signs we will also see in the United Kingdom and Japan. But in the American case the campaign was intensified by wider changes in the political system. This was not only an 'age of scandal' in financial services. In the years during and after Watergate it was an age of scandal in American public life. Some of the changes in the politics of financial regulation were indeed directly due to Watergate: in the mid and late 1970s the previously esoteric issue of accounting standards (an area of regulation which in the 1930s the SEC had simply handed over to private interests) became a subject of ferocious argument because of Watergate-linked revelations about misuse of corporate funds.[93] More generally, out of Watergate came an intense and wide-ranging hunt for scandal by ambitious campaigning journalists. In the 1980s, to take a single instance, political careers were routinely destroyed as a result of revelations about private sexual behaviour. The intense concern with the sexual lives of politicians bore resemblances to the treatment of insider trading: both are transgressions whose nature can be understood by even the dimmest voter; both violate widely held – though not necessarily widely practised

– notions about proper behaviour; and both are so common that there are no difficulties in finding scapegoats.

6 CONCLUSION: CRISIS, SCANDAL AND REGULATION

The bias to meso-corporatism in American financial regulation reflected the contradictory needs of business interests in a pluralist democracy: on the one hand business needed authoritative regulation to prevent excessive competition, abuses and scandals; on the other hand, it needed freedom from the interventionist attentions of a democratic state. Meso-corporatism solved the problem by spiriting regulation into arenas where business interests could expect to have a powerful voice – into 'non-political' agencies and into a network of self-regulatory bodies. The arrangements were legitimised by an ideology of practitioner-based regulation. The hegemony of that ideology was explicable by the historical timing of the most important crisis in the history of the regulatory system, that succeeding the Wall Street Crash in 1929. There is a symmetry to this history, because the hegemony that was created by one crisis was destroyed by another. By the late 1960s structural change – an inevitable outcome of the ceaseless struggle for advantage in markets – had seriously destabilised the balance of interests in the meso-corporatist system. Disaffected interests created dissenting coalitions, sought allies in the wider political system and appropriated ideologies, like anti-trust, capable of challenging established interests and established beliefs. The ideology of practitioner-based regulation was no longer granted automatic acceptance. Meso-corporatism had to demonstrate its practical effectiveness in a society containing numerous social agents ready to seize on regulatory defects as evidence of failure and abuse. The system became, and remains, scandal ridden. The age of the financial services revolution was thus simultaneously an age of great structural change, an age of scandal, and an age when meso-corporatist arrangements became more codified, formally organised and juridified.

These effects were more than domestic, though the domestic setting has dominated this chapter. The financial services revolution was a world-wide experience involving the global integration of markets. But integration could not be symmetrical in nature. The most important feature of the international system was, and remains, the great economic, political and military power of the United States. The international integration of financial markets meant the (partial) Americanisation of financial markets. The United States exported the main features of the financial services revolution: structural change; vulnerability to scandal; the reorganisation of meso-corporatism. The nation most affected by this was Britain – a country where financial politics and foreign economic policy were both uniquely sensitive to American influences. It is thus fitting that we next examine the financial services revolution in the United Kingdom.

3 The United Kingdom: Meso-corporatism and Industrial Decline

> The resistance which comes from interests threatened by an innovation in the productive process is not likely to die out as long as the capitalist order persists.

1 INTRODUCTION

London's importance as an international financial centre far outstrips the international significance of the wider British economy. This financial eminence has many foundations, but the most significant lie in the banking community: London's place in the world financial system rests, above all, on its continuing eminence as an international banking centre. (The extent of this eminence can be seen at a glance by referring back to Table 1 on p. 3). This leading position is traceable to many factors: to the accident of language, because in a century when English has been the world language London possessed a natural advantage over, especially, European rivals; to the equally accidental geographical consideration that has placed London in a 'time zone' intermediate between the two other great centres of New York and Tokyo; to a long history as an economic capital, which endowed London with the commercial and physical infrastructure needed to support markets; to the country's enviable history of political stability; and to the simple fact that for the American bankers who led the first wave of international banking, London was a congenial place in which to live.

All these factors help explain London's important position, but they do not encompass the single most important consideration. By the end of the nineteenth century the City was already the greatest world financial centre – a greatness founded on sterling's role as an international currency, the nation's imperial connections and the international might of British firms. In the years up to the First World War this supremacy was first challenged, and then eclipsed, by New York; and after the War London's international significance was greatly diminished.[1] The 'revival' since 1945 is due to the location of the original Eurodollar markets in London; and this location was in turn the result of a conscious act of policy by the Bank of England, the state agency responsible for banking regulation. The Bank welcomed the Euromarkets to London, its informal system of banking supervision proving a particular attraction to American houses.[2] In short, London's eminence is due, above all, to the policy pursued by the state agency chiefly responsible for the organisation of financial markets in the City. British banking regulation contrasted markedly with the regulatory systems of other economically advanced nations. It worked by informal agreements and understandings, emphasised flexibility in rule making and operated almost totally without legal sanctions.[3] For American firms looking to escape the complex legal system built on the reforms of the 1930s, these arrangements were immensely attractive.

Recent economic history produced, however, a distinctive financial structure in London – and it is this structure which explains the nature of London's participation in the world financial services revolution. The important international markets are located in London, but their importance owes comparatively little to British institutions. They trade financial instruments for the most part denominated in currencies other than sterling, and business is dominated by American and Japanese firms.[4]

Alongside these large, highly competitive international markets there existed until the 1980s a domestic financial system – encompassing securities markets, merchant banking and retail-banking – which was dominated by restrictive practices, substantially protected from external•competition, and governed by a system of meso-corporatism loosely coordinated by the Bank of England. The financial services revolution of the 1980s involved significant changes in all these arrangements: in the restrictions on competition; in the relationship between domestic financial markets and the foreign dominated international markets located in London; and in the organisation of meso-corporatism. The history bears some striking similarities to the American experience – an unsurprising observation because the decisive forces of political competition in a pluralist political system, and economic competition in a market economy, are also at work in the British case. But both the political and the economic environments within which financial markets in Britain work are obviously very different from those in the United States. The way competition in markets created new interests, and the way those interests mobilised politically, was influenced by the particular institutional structure and historical origins of financial regulation in Britain.

The decisive British changes happened in the space of a few short years in the 1980s. In that period restrictions on price competition, notably in the domestic securities market, were lifted. This in turn led to major changes in ownership and in trading practices, the result of which was to link British markets closely to the international system, and to transfer the control of numerous British firms into the hands of foreign multinationals. Almost simultaneously the institutional structure of regulation was reorganised in the 1986 Financial Services Act. A dispersed system of meso-corporatism loosely coordinated by the Bank of England was replaced by more elaborately codified, institutionalised and juridified arrangements. These changes plainly resemble many of the American developments described in Chapter 2; but it is rather as if the reforms of the 1930s and of the 1970s had been telescoped into a few short years. The explanation for the speed of change in Britain also resembles our account of the American case. In the succeeding pages I stress again the way the struggle for competitive advantage in markets damaged and transformed the interests entrenched by meso-corporatism, and the way a pluralist, competitive political system allowed disaffected interests to mobilise for change. But in the British case a new theme introduces itself – Americanisation. The revolution in regulation and trading practices in Britain succeeded, and was in large measure a response to, the American reforms; it was also a response to developments in American-dominated international financial markets. Thus the changes in Britain hinge not only on domestic forces; they are also due to the transmission of external influences to the British system.

The remainder of the chapter is organised in a manner similar to the account of the United States. We begin with the institutional structure because it is both a determinant of policy outcomes and, more simply, because we need to understand the institutional changes that have been introduced in recent years. The new institutional structure was, however, shaped by the legacy of past crises and practices – and these historical experiences are examined in Section 3. Sections 4 and 5 perform for the British case the exercise already accomplished for America: they explore the crisis of meso-corporatism, show how and why this led to reform and – through the example of insider dealing – show how the crisis continues to push the system in the direction of more codification, institutionalisation and juridification.

2   THE INSTITUTIONS OF MESO-CORPORATISM

If the dominant feature of the American regulatory structure was its institutional complexity, the dominant feature of the British system is its novelty. The most important arrangements date only from the Financial Services Act of 1986 which, even at the time of writing, is not fully implemented.

The Financial Services Act is the first comprehensive attempt to create a unified, statutorily based system of regulation to replace the dispersed and loosely coordinated corporatist arrangements that previously existed in the financial services sector.[5] The main provisions of the legislation are as follows. The Act creates for the first time a statutory definition of an investment business. The definition of an 'investment' is very wide: it goes beyond 'securities' as conventionally understood – that is, stocks and shares – to include, for instance, most forms of life insurance policy. An enterprise wishing to engage in an investment business must acquire authorisation; failure to do so is a criminal offence. The authorisation procedures determine the new institutional structure created by the Act. The powers to authorise, and to fix the rules governing authorization, lie with the Secretary of State (for Trade and Industry). However, the legislation allows the Secretary of State to delegate powers to a 'Designated Agency'.

It is this system of delegation which accounts for the corporatist character of the new system. The most important institution in this system is, undoubtedly, the Securities and Investments Board (SIB).[6] The Board is a private institution, with the legal status of a limited company. It is organised so as to be close to the financial services sector. It is funded by a levy on the markets; operates from offices in the Royal Exchange, opposite the Bank of England in the heart of the financial district; and its governing body is made up of leading figures from financial services firms. The careers of the first two chairmen also reflect its closeness to the financial community: the founding chairman, Sir Kenneth Berrill, after a distinguished career in Whitehall, was a senior executive of a leading broking firm; his successor, Mr David Walker, was a leading official of the Bank of England and a key participant in the 'City Revolution' (which is described later in this chapter). The staff of the SIB are recruited by the Board and enjoy City, rather than civil service, conditions of employment. In practice the financial services sector has had a great say over the recruitment of personnel – in part because it is the industry itself which is the most important source of qualified people. It is common knowledge, for instance, that the contract of Sir Kenneth Berrill as chairman was not renewed because powerful groups in the City felt that his approach to regulation was too 'legalistic' and 'inflexible' (in other words, too concerned with subjecting the markets to public control).[7]

The SIB is in important respects modelled on the US Securities and Exchange Commission. In the words of the SIB's first chairman: 'the SIB and the SEC in reality stand very close to each other in terms of their powers and duties . . . we shall, to all intents and purposes, be exercising the powers of an SEC in this country'.[8] The British institution is, true, designed to be more responsive to, and more clearly controlled by, private interests; but while the Board is a private institution, it exists to perform public duties, and to exercise statutory powers delegated from the Secretary of State. It is the 'Designated Agency' to which, under the 1986 Act, the Secretary of State has delegated his powers. As the sole designated agency it has four main tasks. First, it has been chiefly responsible for devising 'model rules', both for individual investment businesses and for the specialised self-regulatory agencies (SROs) which will oversee particular parts of the financial services sector. It also has a continuing responsibility for amending these rules. Second, it has a 'policing' role in respect of a range of offences, and can in certain circumstances also initiate prosecutions. A third responsibility involves the licensing and supervision of individual businesses, although the SIB prefers licensing to be done by intermediary 'self regulatory organisations'. It is the authorisation of these SROs that is the fourth function of the Board. Under the Act the designated agency is empowered to delegate in turn the tasks of authorising and supervising individual businesses to the self-regulatory organisations. (The Board also recognises a range of markets, like the International Stock Exchange, as Recognised Investment Exchanges.) This delegation of powers is accompanied by a range of public controls. The most important control is that the appointment of the Board Chairman, and its Governing body, is decided by the Secretary of State, with the Governor of the Bank of England. The Board must also provide an Annual Report to the Secretary of State, who is in turn obliged to lay the Report before Parliament.[9]

The single most important recurrent function of the Securities and Investments Board is the authorisation and supervision of the individual self-regulatory organisations. In effect the Board delegates to these institutions much of the authority which it has received from the Secretary of State. Like the Board, the SROs have a legally private character: they are limited companies; are funded by the subscriptions of their members; and choose their own staff and governing bodies. Yet these are by no means independent, private companies. They are agencies of the state. Their rules must be approved by the Securities and Investments Board; and in practice the Board's model rules have shaped the constitution of the individual SROs, and it has a decisive say over the most important appointments to the organisations. The SROs are the central feature of the institutional structure of financial regulation in Britain. An individual firm in effect acquires a licence to operate by being accepted into membership of the appropriate SRO. The Securities and Investments Board currently recognises five. Their range and membership show just how radical is the institutional structure created by the Financial Services Act. The largest

SRO, with a staff of over 100 and a membership of over 8000 firms, is the FIMBRA (Financial Intermediaries, Managers and Brokers Regulatory Association).[10] The membership of FIMBRA is swollen by the large numbers of small firms who, as middlemen, sell investment products to the public. The membership and jurisdiction of FIMBRA overlaps with that of a second SRO, the Life Assurance and Unit Trust Regulatory Organisation (LAUTRO), which regulates principally those selling life insurance and unit trusts to the general public. The FIMBRA and LAUTRO are chiefly responsible for ensuring the protection of investors in the mass market for investment products. By contrast a third SRO, the Association of Futures Brokers and Dealers (AFBD) licences and supervises about 250 firms in the highly specialised markets in commodities and futures, where investors are professionals.[11] The Securities Association (TSA) was largely created from the old regulatory arm of the Stock Exchange, while the Investment Managers Regulatory Organisation (IMRO) specialises in the regulation of investment fund managers.[12]

While this system is hardly operational at the present time, its most important feature is nevertheless clear: it is a regulatory structure guided by corporatist principles.[13] Both the Securities and Investments Board, and the individual self regulatory organisations, are private institutions endowed with public duties and exercising legal powers delegated by the state. They now enjoy, in a quintessentially corporatist manner, a monopoly of control over entry to the key financial markets; and in return for this monopoly they are required by the state to control their members. It is doubtful that the framers of the Financial Services Act have ever read Schmitter, but they have nevertheless succeeded in bringing his famous model of corporatism to life. In financial services regulation Britain now has a system, to use Schmitter's words,

> in which the constituent units are organised into a limited number of singular, compulsory, non-competitive, hierarchically ordered and functionally differentiated categories, recognised or licensed (if not created) by the state and granted a deliberate representational monopoly within their respective categories in exchange for observing certain controls on their selection of leaders and articulation of demands and supports.[14]

The great novelty of these arrangements lies not, however, in their meso-corporatist character. As we shall shortly discover the bias to meso-corporatism has deep historical roots in Britain's financial markets. The novelty lies in the changed organisation of the meso-corporatist system. What was once informal, fragmentary and incomplete is now elaborately codified, systematic and organised into institutions backed by legal powers. This change was produced by a crisis in the old arrangements. To understand the crisis we have to understand those old arrangements – and this is the purpose of Section 3

3   ORIGINS AND EVOLUTION OF MESO-CORPORATISM

The regulatory history of British financial services has been highly varied. At one extreme stand a range of institutions – notably the insurance companies and building societies – whose operations have historically been governed by complex and extensive statutes administered by central government.[15] At the opposite extreme stand a range of institutions in the City of London – such as the Stock Exchange and the elite merchant banks – whose operations traditionally escaped regulation either by statute or by central government in Whitehall.[16]

These differences of regulatory regime reflected a key characteristic of English financial life. Institutions which, like the building societies, were provincial in origins and national in the markets they served, were under the regulatory eye of central government; those institutions that were metropolitan in origins, and international in their business connections, largely escaped the regulatory jurisdiction of the state. By the end of the nineteenth century the City already practised a primitive kind of corporatism. The government of markets was in private hands. There existed a loosely organised, highly independent range of corporatist institutions, like the Stock Exchange and the Corporation of Lloyd's, that united regulatory functions with the task of representing the interests of the markets. This arrangement was supported by a hegemonic ideology of 'self-regulation', an exact parallel to the state of affairs across the Atlantic. As the Stock Exchange put it to a Royal Commission in 1878:

> The existing body of rules and regulations have been formed with much care, and are the result of long experience and the vigilant attention of a body of persons intimately acquainted with the needs and exigences of the community for whom they have legislated. Any attempt to reduce these rules to the limits of the ordinary law of the land, or to abolish all checks and safeguards not to be found in that law, would in our opinion be detrimental to the honest and efficient conduct of business.[17]

The ideology of self-regulation pictured financial regulation as an esoteric job that could be done well only by practitioners in the markets, and would be done badly by politicians or civil servants. Even the central bank remained privately owned and substantially under private control.

After 1914 this privileged system faced two crises – the First World War and the Great Depression. The responses to these shaped both the market practices and the regulatory arrangements that were to last into the 1980s. The War, and its associated political and economic upheavals, produced immense demands and immense problems for the City. London's most important economic functions before 1914 were international, not domestic: City markets acted as a kind of 'switchboard' for the open international economic system. The War damaged that system, while the economic nationalism produced by the Great Depression turned damage into destruction.[18] The War also accelerated New York's eclipse of London as a great world financial centre. Thus the City's international economic roles – the most important reasons for its existence – became less significant. Domestically the War released hostile political forces that challenged the hegemonic ideologies of business and, more immediately, encouraged the state to intervene in City markets. The role of government in the economy became vastly more important, and the state's demands on financial institutions became correspondingly more insistent. At the end of the war the political system became more pluralist and democratic: the signs included a greatly enlarged electorate encompassing the working class, a Labour Party suspicious of business privilege, and a growing range of pressure groups representing both workers and industrial manufacturers. The City, by contrast, was still dominated by financial oligarchies hostile to popular government, little involved with domestic manufacturing industry and more attuned to the workings of the international financial system than to the management of Britain's troubled domestic economy.[19]

If this privileged world of regulation was to survive it needed a Praetorian Guard to protect it from the emerging system of pluralist politics. The importance of the Bank of England lies in the fact that for half a century it performed that role.

By 1914 the Bank was already established as the prototypical 'central bank'. It owed this position to a succession of nineteenth-century banking crises. These crises were themselves the outcome of struggles for comparative advantage in markets. The Bank's role was to act as lender of last resort in banking panics, and to organise the rescue of institutions that, through overreaching themselves in competitive struggles, threatened to collapse and, by collapsing, to damage confidence in the whole banking system. (It performed the latter function, most famously, in the crisis that threatened the House of Baring in 1890.) By 1914, therefore, the Bank was already experienced in the job of defending financial interests from the destructive consequences of competitive struggles. Its influence in the City and in Whitehall was nevertheless limited to a narrow, albeit important, range of banking matters. It was still a small and rather amateurish institution run by a part-time Court of Directors drawn mostly from the aristocracy of merchant banking. There were no powerful permanent officials to match those in the Whitehall elite, and the Governor was a fixed term (two year) appointee drawn from the ranks of the part-time members of the Court.[20]

The transformation of the Bank's role was a functional response to the crisis created by the Great War and by the dangerous democratic forces unleashed during and immediately after the War. The Bank's new importance as the manager of City interests was marked by the emergence (as a permanent governor) of Montague Norman, a strange mesmeric figure who typified financial power in the inter-war years. Under Norman the Bank came to occupy a key position, as the voice of the City oligarchies in Whitehall, and as the regulator of the City. Although its influence naturally varied – strongest in banking, weaker on the Stock Exchange, weakest of all in the insurance markets – it was the key to the whole system of self-regulation. Although plainly performing public functions, it remained a privately owned institution. It cultivated, under Norman and his immediate successors, an anti-bureaucratic style and stood between the City and the statute book, resisting legal control by the state in the name of flexibility and informality. During the 1930s, in the face of the Great Depression, the Bank consolidated and extended the network of corporatist institutions in order to cope with the competitive difficulties produced by the economic crisis.[21]

Much of the corporatist system created in the inter-war years endured until the 1980s. It involved a rejection of legal controls, on the grounds of their 'rigidity' and 'inflexibility'. In banking, for instance, there was no significant banking regulatory law until the Banking Act of 1979. The Stock Exchange governed the heart of the securities industry largely as a private corporation. Lloyd's regulated its affairs mostly free of legal controls. Regulation worked through a coordinated system of corporatism, the coordinator being the Bank of England. Many of the associations in the industry had not evolved autonomously; they had been created at the Bank's desire. Representation and regulation were fused: the associations and institutions in City markets had authority because they were recognised by the Bank; and because of this they were able to operate restrictive practices benefiting their members.

This non-legal and economically restrictive system produced a consensual style of regulation – a style identified by Vogel as characteristically British.[22] The oligarchies controlling City markets exercised substantial power, underwritten by the Bank, to exclude 'undesirables' and to enforce conformity upon those allowed into markets. This power was exercised confidentially rather than in open argument – thus keeping regulation private in an age of democratic politics.

The system of regulation established under the guiding hand of the Bank of England depended heavily on restricting competition in both the economic marketplace and in the political marketplace. Such arrangements, we saw in the American case, are highly vulnerable in capitalist democracies. In Britain the system nevertheless proved to be astonishingly durable. It survived the Depression; withstood the extraordinary demands of the wartime economy between 1939 and 1945 and the social and economic reconstruction of the post-war years; and persisted in the long post-war debate about British economic decline. Nevertheless, even before the great climacteric of the 1980s evolutionary changes were taking place that were subjecting the system to growing stress. These changes both anticipated much of what was to happen in the 'City Revolution' and were part of the conditions that made the Revolution possible. They involved alterations in both the nature of City regulation, and in the political environment within which the City functioned. There took place an incremental juridification and codification of the regulatory system. Small though each change was, the totality amounted to an increasing movement of law into financial services. The signs included successive companies acts; the Banking Act of 1979; and contentious legislation reforming the regulatory system in Lloyd's. This process of juridification was itself in part due to the fact that, from the late 1950s, City markets became increasingly prone to 'scandals'.[23]

One of the most striking examples of this process was provided by the regulation of take overs and mergers. There exist obvious competing rights in any take over, not all of which are easily reconcilable: between buyers and sellers, those with property rights in the enterprise, those with rights by virtue of their commitments as employees, and those who have claims as consumers. In Anglo-American capital markets the claims of owners – over managers, workers or consumers – have been paramount. In the last three decades take-over battles have been at the heart of competitive struggles in the United Kingdom, and their regulation thus illustrates to perfection the problems faced in managing conflicts between interests. In the wider economy structural change has been accomplished to a substantial degree through take overs. The stakes in these battles are high: for managers of targets the result of a victorious take over can be loss of jobs; for the bidder, the rewards are enhanced size, market share and, in many cases, the opportunity to dispose of assets (or to strip assets) in the acquired concern.

Among financial services firms the struggle for mergers and acquisition business has been one of the fiercest arenas of competitive struggle, the prizes including the substantial fees for managing attack or defence in a contested take over, and the enhanced business reputation accruing to firms who manage the victor's case in highly publicised battles.[24]

This incentive structure helps explain the ferocity of take-over battles in London in recent decades, and why their regulation has been a perpetual source of trouble. In the 1950s a series of fiercely contested take overs, in which numerous wild claims were made by the competing parties, led to the formation, under pressure from the Bank of England, of a City Working Party drawn from the major institutions. This Working Party produced, in 1959, a set of 'Notes' for guidance in take-over contests. The Notes represented a small increase in the degree to which the regulatory arrangements were codified, but 'no arrangements were made for the observance of the notes to be supervised'.[25] In other words, an incremental growth in codification had not been matched by any corresponding increase in institutionalisation or juridification.

It is perhaps no surprise that the 'Notes' failed to stamp out the abuses and scandals caused by competitive struggles. These were highlighted by a renewed bout of take overs in the mid-1960s. In 1967 the City Working Party was revived, and in the next year produced two significant reforms. First, a more precise and elaborate 'City Code' replaced the old 'Notes': in other words, there was a further increase in codification. Second, a Panel on Take Overs and Mergers was established, with a permanent staff, to administer and interpret the Code: in other words, there was a clear growth of institutionalisation. These reforms still did not solve the problem of control. Since the early 1970s take-over activity in the City has been the source of recurrent public scandals, involving allegations of practices like asset stripping and insider trading. (The significance of these is considered in more detail in Section 5.) Coping with these scandals has involved developing an increasingly complex and contested City Code. This process has culminated in a partial juridification of the system: the courts now hold the proceedings of the Panel to be subject to judicial review, while compliance with Panel decisions is one of the conditions of SRO membership under the Financial Services Act.[26]

The significance of the recent history of take-over regulation is, therefore, that it illustrates the connection between growing codification, juridification and institutionalism, on the one hand, and competitive struggles and 'scandal' on the other.

The slow changes in the practice of regulation even before the City Revolution of the 1980s were in turn connected to another gradual development:

a decline in the political autonomy of the City. The most important sign of this was the changing role of the Bank of England in the two decades after the publication of the Radcliffe *Report* in 1959. The changing role of the Bank, and the implications of this change for the political autonomy of the City, are a vital part of the background to the events of the 1980s. The Bank, we have seen, acted after the First World War as a Praetorian Guard protecting the City from the newly developing forces of pluralist democracy. But with any Praetorian guard there exists an obvious danger – that the guardian will itself develop the capacity and the ambition to govern. Until the end of the 1950s this danger was averted. The evidence to the Bank Rate Tribunal in 1957, and to the Radcliffe Committee a short time afterwards, showed the Bank to be still a quintessentially 'City' institution: closer to the markets than to government, run more like a City firm than a public agency, and dominated by figures drawn from the City elite.[27] The Bank had been transferred to public ownership in 1946, but this had produced little alteration in either its relations with Government or in its regulatory style. In the 1950s the state's relations with the financial markets still resembled those existing before the Second World War: they were mediated through the Bank; they were informal and non-legal; and they were organised into a series of corporatist institutions dominated, for the most part, by socially select oligarchies.[28]

The nationalisation of the Bank in 1946, though it had a largely symbolic purpose at the time, nevertheless over a span of three decades helped change the character of the institution. The report of the Radcliffe Committee advocated a more professionally organised central bank, and one more closely integrated with the machinery of economic policy making in Whitehall.[29] The Governor of the time had originally dismissed such notions with the remark that he preferred 'a Bank and not a study-group', but in the two decades after 1960 important changes in its character nevertheless took place.[30] The Bank began increasingly to acquire the characteristics of a public institution. Following the Radcliffe proposals for greater coordination of monetary and fiscal policy, it became more closely integrated into the Whitehall policy-making machinery. It was also more closely integrated into the public sector: Parliament began to scrutinise its operations, and in a traumatic period at the end of the 1960s the Bank's residual assumptions about its independence from the state were publicly challenged by a Parliamentary enquiry.[31] At the same time as the Bank was shedding many of the remnants of its 'private' past, its internal structure was also altering. After 1960 it became a much more formally organised and professional body, in which personal contacts with the markets became less important, and economic analysis became more so. The *Quarterly*

Bulletin – the first sign of a serious commitment to rigorous economic analysis – began publication in 1960. Executive (full-time) directors on the Court became more influential at the expense of the once supreme part-timers. The ascendancy of the Bank professionals was symbolised by the appointment as Governor of Leslie O'Brien, the first full-time employee of the Bank to reach that position. Although O'Brien's two successors have been outsiders, it is the permanent professionals who have continued decisively to guide the Bank – a factor that was decisively to influence its role in the changes of the 1980s.

The City's relations with the state therefore altered gradually in the decades after World War Two because its traditional mediator, the Bank of England, ceased to be an appendage of the City, and became an independent institution increasingly controlled by its own professional staff. The character of regulatory relationships between the Bank and the City also altered. Regulation through a collection of informal, dispersed corporatist institutions began to be replaced by more formal arrangements. The most important of these changes were the result of the great banking crisis of the mid-1970s. In the years between 1974 and 1979 the central bank abandoned a traditional, informal and unsystematic system of supervision for a more detailed and elaborate set of rules administered by a professional staff of regulators backed by legal powers.[32]

The evolution of the Bank of England from a City institution to an institution that regulated the City was, we will shortly see, of exceptional importance to the reforms of the 1980s. By the beginning of that decade the Bank itself had won a partial autonomy from the interests inside the financial markets, and was in a position to develop policy objectives in some degree independent of those interests. The objectives to which it became committed were influenced by a wide range of factors: by its own institutional interest in remaining a leading world financial regulator, a position that in turn depended on London's prominence as a world financial centre; by the need to respond to the demands of bureaucratic politics in Whitehall; and even by the needs of strategically placed professionals inside the Bank to advance their careers by promoting innovatory policies. In brief, the Bank that emerged after the First World War as the guardian of the City elite against a potentially democratic state had now itself become, to some degree, an institution of that state.

The historical background to the 'City Revolution' is plainly very different from the historical background to the changes in American financial markets. The crises that gave birth to the system; the actual structure of markets; the political culture and the political institutions surrounding financial regulation: all these had a distinctive British flavour.

Yet the forces that drove the system were in many ways remarkably alike on both sides of the Atlantic. Financial regulation in both Britain and the United States was strongly biased towards meso-corporatism. This bias was a functional response to the need to solve problems that likewise were remarkably similar in both countries: regulating struggles for competitive advantage so that they did not endanger the foundations of the market order; integrating the new interests constantly created by the outcomes of competitive struggles; and insulating the markets from the pressures of democracy. These problems proved more intractable in the United States than in Britain because both American capitalism and American democracy are more vigorous than their British counterparts. Still, by the start of the 1980s the British system had been driven to the brink of revolutionary change. This revolution is our next concern.

4   THE CITY REVOLUTION AND THE CRISIS
   OF MESO-CORPORATISM

By the end of the 1970s meso-corporatist regulation in the City had reached a critical point: critical in the everyday sense that there existed a widespread perception that there were serious problems in maintaining the City's place as a leading world financial centre; and critical in the narrow sense that regulation was at a momentous turning point. The 1980s were to be dominated by what is colloquially called 'the City revolution'.

That revolution had three aspects.[33] The first concerned the actual structure of the regulatory system, and need only detain us a moment because we have already described it in Section 2 of this chapter. In the Financial Services Act, 1986, meso-corporatism was juridified, codified and formally organised. A second aspect involved widespread changes in competitive practices. By the end of the 1970s many City markets were already highly competitive: they included the Euromarkets, and large areas of banking that had been freed from controls as long ago as the early 1970s. But in the chief domestic securities markets limits on price competition and on market entry remained in force. In the space of three years after 1983 there took place substantial changes in these market practices. The most important included the phasing out of limits to price competition on the Stock Exchange, the abolition of rules separating firms acting as principals in trading from those acting as brokers, and the ending of prohibitions on the sale of Stock Exchange firms to outsiders.[34] These changes paved the way for the third major feature of the City Revolution, a transformation of ownership structures. Until the

1980s firms in the domestic securities industry were, characteristically, small, independent British-owned concerns, often run as partnerships. In a few short years after 1983 the most important became subsidiaries of multinational conglomerates, many foreign owned, operating across the financial services sector. The scale of this change is remarkable: between 1983 and 1986, 105 stock exchange member firms were the subject of outside participation in ownership; and over 30 of these involved foreign concerns.[35] The three faces of the City Revolution – the reconstruction of corporatism, the abolition of many restrictions on competitive struggles and the transformation of ownership – are all closely connected. Explaining why they came about, and why they came about so swiftly in the 1980s, has to begin by describing the chain of events that led to the changes.

The critical revolutionary moment happened in July 1983 with the 'Goodison/Parkinson' agreement – an agreement to reform competitive practices on the Stock Exchange, concluded by Nicholas Goodison, the Chairman of the Stock Exchange and Cecil Parkinson, at that time Secretary of State. But the origins go back a decade earlier, to the Fair Trading Act of 1973. This legislation strengthened the law against restrictive practices in Britain and, in the Office of Fair Trading, established a highly influential institutional advocate of ideologies of free competition. The OFT's jurisdiction was significantly widened in January 1976 by a Statutory Instrument (the Restrictive Trade Practices, Services, Order) extending the scope of fair-trading law to service industries. The Order thus immediately brought a wide range of financial institutions, the most important of which was the Stock Exchange, under the regulatory authority of the Office of Fair Trading, and of its Director General, Gordon Borrie. The Director General, an adept publicist and a shrewd manipulator in the bureaucratic politics of regulatory change, was to prove a formidable critic of City markets. The immediate effects of the Order were to oblige the Stock Exchange to register its rule book with the OFT; to require the reform of any offending rules; and, failing an agreement on reform, to require the OFT to bring the rule book for judgement before the Restrictive Practices Court.[36]

The Stock Exchange Council's response to this challenge was two-fold: to attempt escape from the clutches of the OFT; and, in the event of that attempt failing, to mount a comprehensive legal defence of the rule book. In the late 1970s the Council, supported at the highest levels by the Bank of England, lobbied the Labour Secretary of State for Prices and Consumer Protection (Mr Hattersley) for exemption from the 1976 order.[37]

This attempt failed. It is a truism that affected interests have the best chance of influencing policy before government commits itself publicly. Once the original Order was published, hardly any administration was likely to agree to special pleading and was even less likely to retreat when it was a Labour Administration suspicious of City interests. The final acknowledgement that the Exchange's and the Bank's lobbying had failed came after a meeting with Ministers on 8 February 1979. On the following day Mr Hattersley's Minister of State told the Commons that the Exchange would not be exempted from the Order, and in the same month the Director General gave notice that he was referring the Exchange's rule book to the Restrictive Practices Court.[38]

The return of the Conservatives to office in May 1979 gave renewed hope that the Exchange might escape the clutches of the OFT. That hope was an illusion; despite a repetition of representations from the Council and from the Bank, two successive Secretaries of State – Mr Nott and Mr Biffen – declined to amend the original Order.[39] By June 1983, when the Conservatives were of course returned with a greatly increased majority, the Exchange had turned most of its energies to preparing a detailed defence of its rule book for the Restrictive Practices Court. The first hearings were scheduled for January 1984, and at the moment of the Conservatives' victory witnesses' proofs were in the final stages of preparation.[40] Mrs Thatcher's choice as Secretary of State in the new Administration, Cecil Parkinson, lasted only until the following October, when private troubles forced his resignation; but his brief tenure was momentous for the Exchange and for the future of London as a financial centre.

On assuming office Parkinson saw, in quick succession, the Director General of the OFT and Nicholas Goodison of the Stock Exchange. At the meeting with Goodison the Secretary of State offered the concession for which the Exchange had long lobbied: exemption from the jurisdiction of the OFT. In return the Exchange would have to amend key rules to which the Office of Fair Trading had objected. After discussions with Council members, Goodison in turn offered a set of concessions which, adopted unanimously by Council on July 22, were announced by Parkinson in the House of Commons four days later. The critical proposals were as follows: minimum commissions on bargains were to be abolished by December 1986; there were to be lay representatives on the Council of the Exchange; a new internal appeal procedure was to be established; the substance of rule changes was to be decided in agreement with the Bank of England; and the implementation of the whole package of reforms was to be monitored by a group drawn from the Bank and the DTI. In return the Government committed itself to seek Parliamentary approval exempting the Stock Exchange from the restrictive practices legislation.[41] Borrie publicly protested against the 'blow to the Office' (of fair trading), declined voluntarily to withdraw the Office's case against the Exchange, and thus obliged the Government to introduce immediate legislation extricating the Exchange from the clutches of the OFT and the Restrictive Practices Court.[42]

The most important item in the Goodison/Parkinson Agreement was the decision to phase out minimum commissions on bargains (an exact parallel to the decision made in New York in 1975). The significance of the item was two-fold. First, it removed the major barrier to price competition; second, in a manner again paralleling the American experience, by removing this restriction it intensified the wider competitive struggle and led to far reaching structural changes. The two most important restrictions formally untouched by the agreement were 'single capacity', the enforced separation of brokers (agents for buyers and sellers of stock) and jobbers (dealers as principals); and a Stock Exchange rule prohibiting outsiders from holding more than a minority stake in member firms. Within a few months of the original agreement the Stock Exchange Council had prepared plans to abolish both these restrictions.[43] The abolition of single capacity was not at all unexpected: Goodison himself told Parkinson at the time of the agreement that the separation of brokers and jobbers would not survive the intensified competition produced by the abolition of minimum commissions.[44] Thus the agreement of July 1983 represents a decisive moment in the revolution of trading practices: a moment when the competitive struggle intensified, sweeping away the restrictions embodied in single capacity and leading within a few years to the transfer of a large part of the domestic securities industry into foreign hands.

The events of the summer of 1983 also transformed opinions about the regulatory framework for financial services. In 1983 there already existed a blueprint for reform, but it commanded little support in the City. Following the collapse of firms advising investors in high-risk securities, the Department of Trade and Industry had commissioned from Professor L. Gower, the country's leading authority on company law, a review of the system of investor protection. Gower's first Report, published in 1982, received a hostile reception in the City, despite the fact that it proposed only modest reforms, leaving decisive control in the hands of City institutions like the Council for the Securities Industry.[45] But his second report, published in 1984 after extensive consultation, both resembled the final shape of the Financial Services Act and was received much more favourably by the City elite.[46] The reason for its favourable reception was that the intensification of competitive struggles signalled by the Goodison/Parkinson agreement had, by transforming the rules of business conduct in markets, made the creation of a new regulatory framework an urgent necessity.

The core of Gower's proposals – that entry to the industry should depend on a system of licencing, that the administration of this system should be delegated by law to a range of self-regulatory organisations, and that these agencies should in turn be controlled by a single supervisory body – resurfaced in the 1985 White Paper containing the Government's initial proposals for financial regulation, and in the 1986 legislation itself.[47] By the beginning of 1984 the most powerful voices in the City had moved from the 'dismissal' of Gower voiced two years earlier to endorsement of his scheme, with one significant qualification. In Gower's report, while the self-regulatory agencies would have had a semi-public status, the supervisor of the whole system would have been a public body, either a central government department or a free-standing commission (Gower preferred the latter, but believed the government was more likely to adopt the former). This was widely rejected in the City – not surprisingly, since the single most important thread in the history of City regulation has been a determination to preserve its autonomy from the state.[48] The most powerful interests in the City were clear in their opposition to a statutory commission. They were less than clear about their positive preferences. Structural change in the markets was accelerating, and in accelerating was destabilising traditional alliances between interests. The creation of a coalition supporting clear proposals was thus immensely difficult. The Council for the Securities Industry debated the issues, and could not agree on the status and powers of a regulator.[49] In May 1984 the Governor announced the formation of a Group, drawn from the great and the good of the City, to advise him on the details of reform. It is clear from the Group's terms of reference that the markets were to be given a veto over any proposal for a public agency, for the Group was to advise on a structure which would 'attract sufficient support from potential participants to be capable of early implementation'.[50]

This group is often credited with inventing the solution eventually adopted – the creation of a public/private regulator, legitimised by the language of 'practitioner regulation'.[51] We cannot know this for certain, because the Group's report was never published. It is actually more likely that its members simply reproduced the differences between existing interests: it even contained, in the person of David Hopkinson, part of a radical minority who were opposed root-and-branch to the reforms introduced after the Goodison/Parkinson agreement. The authoritative decision had to await the appearance in January 1985 of the White Paper on *Financial Services in the United Kingdom*. This laid out what is today the structure of the Financial Services Act. The fundamental principle was 'self-regulation within a statutory framework': the creation of a private sector body to whom statutory powers are delegated.[52]

The explanation for this solution lies not in the power of any confidential advisory group; it resides in a mixture of ideological assumptions and situational contingency. Almost everybody favoured practitioner-based or self-regulation, though equally almost everybody conceived of this in different ways. There was no interest inside the DTI or the Bank of England in taking on the horrifyingly complex task of creating and controlling the details of the new system. The Government was supposed to be cutting the size of the public sector, and earlier in the decade had made a point of culling 'quangos'. A private institution with public powers gave City interests the hope that they could still control the system, kept the cost out of the public purse, kept the personnel recruited off the public sector manpower totals, and hived the appallingly complex detailed tasks off from central government. It was a solution riddled with ambiguities and contradictions produced by a coalition of interests itself founded on contradiction and ambiguity.

Much of importance was to happen after the appearance of the White Paper. With its publication, however, corporatism was preserved, if only in a more codified, juridified and institutionalised form. The White Paper's appearance was a major turning point, and it is appropriate that we now move from narrative to an analysis of the forces that drove the system to the point of rapid and unexpected reform in the early and mid-1980s. The elements include features already familiar from our analysis of the American financial services revolution: the twin effects of competitive struggles in markets and the demands on regulatory bodies to manage these struggles.

By the late 1970s, when the Office of Fair Trading was beginning to exert pressure for reform, structural change in the financial markets had already damaged the interests traditionally in control of institutions like the Stock Exchange; had created doubts about the very viability of existing trading practices; and had brought to prominence new institutions with interests different from those of the elites entrenched in the traditional system of meso-corporatism. The result was a continuing debate within the financial community about the need for change, and the slow creation of a coalition of reformers.

One important structural change exactly paralleled the American experience. By the 1970s the once dominant private shareholder owned only a minority of securities. The largest blocks were controlled by financial institutions like insurance companies and pension funds, who could see from the American experience after 1975 that competitive commissions would result in discounts for the big institutional customers. By the end of the 1970s the Stock Exchange was looking increasingly anachronistic: the numbers of jobbing firms – who supposedly competed to make markets in stocks – had been so reduced by defensive mergers that in important sectors it was difficult to see any evidence of competition; the broking partnerships were, by international standards, tiny and undercapitalised; and in a world where technical innovation was integrating markets world wide, the technological resources and trading practices of the domestic securities markets were antiquated.[53]

The pressure for reform intensified with the abolition of exchange controls in 1979. Abolition was both a response to the increasingly global character of markets, and an additional stimulus to that process of global integration. After 1979, the British securities industry no longer operated in a protected, domestic arena; it was a small declining part of ferociously competitive world markets.[54] London's survival as a significant trading centre depended on full integration into these markets, and that in turn entailed the destruction of traditional regulation. The structural changes both at home and abroad had, by the end of the decade, begun to mobilise interests favouring reform. The big British and foreign multinational banks, and the US and Japanese brokerage houses, were anxious to destroy barriers to entry to the British securities industry as part of a world-wide expansion of their operations. The large domestic institutional investors were, like their American counterparts a decade or so earlier, resentful at the large, effortless profits creamed by the brokers inside the Stock Exchange price cartel. The more ambitious and efficient of the Exchange's own members saw integration with large multinational conglomerates as their only hope of competing in the world securities industry. Those, like Goodison, who were concerned with the institutional health and the collective interest of the Stock Exchange, became increasingly anxious about the robustness of the jobbing system. As early as 1977, for instance, the Committee of Senior Partners (on the Exchange) had warned that the reduction in the numbers of jobbing firms, problems of maintaining adequate capital and pressure on profit margins all made the system highly vulnerable.[55] From the late 1970s onwards there were frequent debates inside the Stock Exchange Council, with supporters of reform urging change in a wide range of restrictive practices.[56]

It is, however, extremely unlikely that these reforms would have happened spontaneously; state compulsion was needed. Corporatism had created an economically privileged group of Stock Exchange members, largely insulated from price competition, enjoying for the most part a leisurely and opulent existence. The necessary reforms required amendments to the Stock Exchange constitution, in some cases demanding a 75 per cent majority.[57] This was hardly going to happen without some fierce external pressure, when even the dimmest broker could see that similar reforms in New York after 1975 had created a dangerously competitive environment. At the end of the decade the interests in the City were effectively deadlocked over the question of reform.

This, then, was the background to the intervention by the Office of Fair Trading. The OFT's role should be understood as a sign that the City's political independence and its ideology of self-regulation were under challenge. The year 1976 was a critical moment, when the Exchange lobbied unsuccessfully for exemption from the Order extending restrictive practices legislation to services.[58] The Exchange was an ineffective lobbyist, not because of the stupidity of individuals but because the institution suffered from a historically conditioned political incompetence. The ideology of self-regulation meant that in the past institutions like the Stock Exchange did not have to argue for exemption from state controls. It was just assumed that they had the right to guide their own affairs. By the 1970s, when the Exchange was actually required to make its case in Whitehall, it had little experience of how to do the job.

The Exchange's difficulties were compounded by the fact that the OFT represented not only an alien institutional intrusion, but also an alien ideological challenge. We saw in the American case that Wall Street was damaged because the pluralistic character of American society created ideologies like 'anti-trust' which were capable of challenging its claims to political independence. The OFT represented a similar, though more muted, ideological challenge. The creation of the OFT was the culmination of a run of anti-restrictive practices legislation in Britain. This legislation was prompted in part by the country's economic decline, and by the belief in some elite groups that the state should compel the business community to compete more effectively. By the 1970s ideologies of free competition and fair trading had penetrated key elites. They included sections of the commercial bar, such as judges in the Restrictive Practices Court; leading civil servants in the Department of Trade and Industry; and social democratic modernisers, like Gordon Borrie and the Labour ministers who in the late 1970s turned down the Stock Exchange's belated plea for exemption from restrictive practices legislation. The ideology had even penetrated the elite of the Conservative Party, the City's traditional political ally. That is why, after 1979, the Exchange still could not escape the clutches of the OFT, even though it faithfully turned up on the doorstep to put its case to successive Conservative ministers.

By 1982 the Exchange was in the last stages of preparing to put an elaborate and costly defence of its rule book to the Restrictive Practices Court. By then, however, it was recognised, even by defenders of the old order, that the judgement was likely to be unfavourable.[59] At this point there occurred the decisive event leading to the revolutionary changes of 1983: the Bank of England deserted the Exchange. Until then the Bank, despite its doubts, had supported the Exchange's pleas to be exempted from Borrie's jurisdiction. Two immediate events caused the change: the abolition of exchange controls in 1979 which, by hastening the global integration of markets, made the Bank's officials sensitive to the challenge to London's leading position from other financial centres; and the appointment in 1982 of David Walker as Bank director with responsibility for City organisation.[60] But these were only a sign of more fundamental forces. As we saw in Section 3 of this chapter the Bank, originally the protector of the City elite against the state, had by the 1970s ceased to be a reliable guardian. It had become a governing institution, and had even been itself penetrated by the ideologies of fair trading and free competition that influenced other governing elites. It shared with those elites concern over Britain's economic decline, an obvious consideration in worries about foreign challenges to London's position as a leading financial centre. The Bank's power and prestige both within the British state and internationally rested on its position as the regulator of a world financial capital. In short, by the 1980s it had its own ideology and institutional interests and there was no good reason why it should subordinate those to the demands of an inefficient domestic securities industry.

Mr Walker's role emphasises the growth of the Bank's independence. He is perhaps the single most important figure in the City revolution: the shift of Bank policy in 1982 was signalled by informal discussions held by Walker in Whitehall; after the Goodison/Parkinson agreement he was important in mobilising City support for the reforms, and in encouraging many of the changes of ownership after 1983;[61] and when Sir Kenneth Berrill offended too many powerful City interests it was Mr Walker who replaced him as Chairman of the SIB. But Walker is himself only a sign of how far the Bank, by the 1980s, was controlled by a full-time officialdom governed by the usual mix of institutional pressures and the need to make a career. As someone spoken of as a possible future Governor, Walker in 1982 had an obvious need to make a mark by sponsoring innovative policies. (A similar process can be seen in the reorganisation of the gilt-edged market after 1983, a reform pushed through by Eddie George, another full time official often publicly mentioned as a future Governor.)

The key forces causing the 'City Revolution' can, in summary, now be described as follows. Meso-corporatism gave power and privileges to elites like those in stockbroking. The elites were unable to suppress the effects of wider competitive struggles. The competitive struggles led to structural change and created the new interests pressing for reform in the late 1970s and early 1980s. The changing character of the state had meanwhile damaged the political mechanisms that allowed the old meso-corporatism to function: the hegemonic ideology of self-regulation was challenged by alternative ideologies of fair trading; elites in the state structure developed the capacity and the inclination to intervene in the City; the Bank of England, operating with a degree of autonomy from particular interests in the markets, pursued policies shaped by its own full time staff.

The 'City revolution' begun by the Goodison/Parkinson agreement thus marks more than a change in economic practices; it is also a sign of profound change in the politics of financial regulation. This explains why meso-corporatism has been reorganised – as we have already seen – in the Financial Services Act. The 1983 agreement had two objectives: to reform trading practices, and to protect the City from control by a state agency. That is why Goodison traded a commitment to reform the Exchange in return for a promise that the Office of Fair Trading would no longer have jurisdiction over it. As one of the Exchange's own officials put it, 'Had the exemption (in the Goodison/Parkinson agreement) not been granted the Stock Exchange would always have had to submit its rules for OFT approval, a process entirely incompatible with the principle of self-regulation.'[62] Yet the agreement, by preparing the way for more competitive struggles in markets, changed the political condition of the financial services sector. The old, autonomous and dispersed network of corporatist institutions, like the Stock Exchange, owed their regulatory power to their ability to confer the privileges of restrictive practices on members. The abolition of these practices meant that a new source of regulatory authority was required. Indeed, as we saw in Section 3, economic change had already undermined the effectiveness of the traditional system.

The decline was illustrated by Professor Gower's inquiry, which was originally occasioned by the collapse of firms licensed by the Department of Trade and Industry at the margin of the regulatory system.[63] But the scope of his enquiry quickly went beyond the narrow matter of the future role of the system of licencing, to a review of the whole system of regulating investment markets. The comprehensive range of Gower's work reflected the growing difficulties experienced in operating the old system even before the Goodison/Parkinson agreement. Gower's own summary of the problems (in his 1982 report) could not be bettered:

Complication, uncertainty, irrationality, failure to treat like alike, inflexibility, excessive control in some areas and too little (or none) in others, the creation of an elite and a fringe, lax enforcement, delays, over concentration on honesty rather than competence, undue diversity of regulations and regulators, and failure overall to achieve a proper balance between Governmental regulation and self-regulation.[64]

In the summer of 1983, therefore, a number of different factors coincided: the old system of meso-corporatist regulation had been damaged by successive scandals and crises; the Goodison/Parkinson agreement meant that new sources of regulatory authority were urgently required; and Gower was at hand to point out the one obvious source of new authority, which was the state. His main Report, completed in 1983 and published the following January, favoured an agency with statutory power supervising a range of semi-public self-regulatory agencies. This report provided the blueprint for the Government's 1985 White Paper on the regulation of financial services and for the final legislation. The only significant part of Gower's model to be rejected was, as we have seen, his preference for a public agency to oversee regulation – because, as we also know, the City's priority was to preserve the political independence conferred by self-regulation.[65]

The Financial Services Act and the 'City Revolution' are thus closely connected. The point of the Act is to renew the regulatory authority which had been damaged by successive scandals, and given the final blow by the removal of many restrictive practices after 1983. The Act renews regulatory authority by using state power – embodied in law – to support the new regulatory agencies. It does this through corporatist agencies – legally private institutions licensed by law to perform public duties. In this way it tries to reconcile the preservation of the City's autonomy from the democratic state with the use of that state's power and legitimacy.

Writing in early 1990, the Act is barely operational, and it is impossible to judge how successfully these two contradictory objectives are being realised. There is certainly ample evidence to support the view that powerful interests in the City have carried out a considerable constitutional coup. The new system – measured by the authority given to its institutions, the resources at their disposal and the coverage of markets – is an immeasurable improvement in regulatory capacity on what went before. Both the SIB and the SROs are substantially protected from the central machinery of the state. Apart from the formal safeguards built into the Act – for instance, their creation as private companies – the practical working of the new system suggests that the institutions are responsive to the interests in the markets, while the staff and the governing bodies of the SIB and the individual SROs are overwhelmingly dominated by practitioners. The failure of Sir Kenneth Berrill to win a second term as SIB Chairman – on the grounds that his conception of regulation was too inflexible and legalistic – was also a victory for those who wished to keep the system under private control, and a defeat for those anxious to move the SIB to the kind of position presently occupied in the United States by the Securities and Exchange Commission.[66]

Against these signs of private control, however, can be seen contradictory signals. The SIB and the SROs are semi-private, but by the same token are semi-public. Many of the powers given to central government – for instance the appointment of Chairman and Board members – represent a historically unprecedented increase in public control over City institutions. The rhetoric widely used to legitimise the system – practitioner-based regulation within a statutory framework – is not easy to reconcile with the evolution of that system since 1983. The complexity of the rules is turning regulation into an activity for specialists – full-time officials in the SIB and the SROs, and full-time specialists in the 'compliance departments' of firms. The Financial Services Act runs to nearly 300 pages; the Prevention of Fraud Act, which it replaced, ran to 20 pages;[67] this is a world away from what practitioner-based regulation used to mean, and is also very different from what many in the City originally envisaged.[68] The new system involves, in brief, a shift towards more juridification, codification and institutionalisation. One of the most important forces continuing to drive it in that direction is scandal. The new system created in the 1980s has failed to alter the history of scandal which, for over two decades, has plagued the City. In recent years scandals have increasingly concerned insider trading. That is our next concern.

5   INSIDER TRADING AND MESO-CORPORATISM

We saw in Chapter 2 that across the Atlantic there is a history of litigation about insider trading stretching back more than three decades, that this litigation culminated in legislation during the 1980s, and that the pursuit of insider dealing continues to produce wave after wave of scandal on Wall Street. The regulation of insider trading in Britain is marked by two features: a history which, in its indifference to the practice, contrasts remarkably with the American experience; but, latterly, a drive against insider trading modelled closely on the recent American patterns and involving increasingly close cooperation with the American authorities. The history of British regulation has progressed through four stages.

First, indifference or even tacit approval; second, disapproval combined with reluctance to legislate against the practice; third, legal prohibitions .:t a reluctance to implement the legislation; finally, and most recently, more stringent legislation, increasingly serious efforts at enforcement and a series of scandals tied, in some instances, to the American cases examined in Chapter 2.

The age of indifference lasted in Britain until the closing years of the 1950s. The courts had historically been almost silent, and when not silent gave tacit approval. The landmark judgement, delivered as long ago as 1902, has been called 'an insider's charter' because it ruled that directors of companies had no fiduciary duty to account to shareholders for profits made by share dealing in their enterprise.[69] It is difficult to obtain anything but anecdotal recollections about the extent of insider dealing in the past, but these anecdotes, combined with the attitude of the courts, suggest that it was a perfectly acceptable practice. The chairman of a large industrial company told me that when he was involved in his first uncontested take over in the 1950s, his opposite number in the target company told him that he had alerted some friends so that they could buy shares in advance of the public announcement of the take over. When my informant protested that this was unethical his counterpart, surprised, remarked that he had after all only told a few friends! A single anecdote by itself proves nothing; but when combined with our knowledge that the City was a series of intimate business communities largely uncontrolled by the courts or by central government, it strengthens the view that insider dealing was a common and acceptable City practice.

The end of this age of indifference coincided with the great take over battles of the late 1950s and early 1960s. As we saw earlier, this period was marked by competitive struggles as new interests tried to challenge those already established under the existing system of meso-corporatism. These take over battles put the City, and its practices, onto the front pages of newspapers and led the City elite to attempt to limit the damage done by competition.[70] It was already a requirement of the 1968 Takeover Code that 'there should be no misuse by an insider of the knowledge that a take-over bid is to be made'.[71] The 'age of disapproval' had begun. It was to last until 1980 and was marked by periodic efforts on the part of regulators, like the Panel on Take Overs and Mergers, and the Stock Exchange, to lay down rules governing insider dealing and to censure those who broke the rules. These efforts failed: the existing system of meso-corporatism possessed neither the resources to detect the practice, nor the authority effectively to punish it.[72] As early as 1973 both the City elite and the Conservative Government had decided that state power was needed. In that year both the Stock Exchange and the Take Over Panel advocated legislation, and in the same year the Government's Companies Bill included measures against insider dealing.[73] This shift of opinion was remarkable at a time when it was still the overwhelming view in the City that self-regulation outside the law was the proper way to run financial markets. The episode shows how competitive struggles were already destroying the old meso-corporatism and causing scandals that endangered the City's independence.

The Heath Government's Companies Bill lapsed when his administration lost office in 1974; a later attempt by the Labour government to legislate was also lost through the intervention of a General Election. It was not until 1980, therefore, that law reached the statute book. The Companies Act of that year prohibited selected classes of insiders – directors, senior employees – from dealing or tipping on the basis of unpublished price sensitive information.[74] The third phase, of ineffective and unenthusiastic enforcement, had begun. Implementation of the new law relied on market surveillance by the Stock Exchange. The Exchange was to report suspect price movements to the Department of Trade and Industry, which in turn was to investigate and decide whether prosecution was to be advised. In the years between 1980–86 only one hundred cases were passed by the Exchange to the Department, resulting in only eight minor prosecutions.[75] Leigh has remarked that 'if ever a topic afforded material for an abusive Marxist thesis, insider trading does'.[76] It was certainly remarkable that a problem which had driven the City elite to the statute book should now be enforced so ineffectively.

This age of ineffective enforcement ended in the mid-1980s, to be succeeded by the present, fourth, phase in the history of insider dealing regulation. This has been marked by renewed legislation, more determined enforcement and a series of highly public scandals reaching to the very heights of the City elite. The Insider Dealing (Company Securities) Act of 1985 already contained renewed measures against the practice, but the most important new provisions are in the 1986 Financial Services Act.[77] The Act strengthened the investigative powers of inspectors appointed by the Secretary of State. At the end of 1986 the timetable for introducing the various measures in the legislation was revised to allow the more rapid implementation of the section dealing with insider trading.[78] This was because the law was passed in the middle of widespread publicity about scandalous City practices. These encompassed the enforced rescue by the authorities in September 1984 of Johnson Matthey, a 'recognised' bank, and an intense campaign in the media and in Parliament against fraud in the markets.[79] In November 1986 insider trading regulation claimed its first significant victim, with the exposure, resignation (and later conviction) of

Mr Geoffrey Collier, the securities chief of a leading City institution.[80]. At the turn of the year the still unresolved Guinness scandal broke, leading to resignations in the company, charges against a number of leading City figures, and accusations of widespread manipulation of share prices in take-over battles.[81] Of course we must be careful not to exaggerate the extent of the changes that took place after 1985. Insider trading in Britain has been criminalised, but it remains a privileged crime. By American standards enforcement and punishment are light: Mr Collier received a one-year suspended prison sentence and a £25,000 fine. Nevertheless the change since the early 1980s – let alone since the indifference of the 1950s – is dramatic.[82] The state has equipped itself with new powers to investigate and punish insider dealing, and has not hesitated to destroy the careers of leading members of the business elite in using those powers. This all shows yet again how inadequately 'deregulation' describes what has been going on in financial markets. The campaign against insider trading is of a piece with other parts of the City revolution: it demonstrates the growing willingness and capacity of the state to intervene in financial services in order to influence the outcome of competitive struggles. It reflects, in Levi's words, 'a broad conception of state interest in the profitability and global reputation of the securities industry'.[83]

Yet we still have to explain why a practice which was so recently the subject of indifference and even tacit approval should quite suddenly be thought to hold the key to London's global reputation. It is not at all clear, for instance, that the institutions whose business really matters if London is to retain its world prominence are actually very troubled by the practice of insider trading. The most formidable foreign group in London, the Japanese, can hardly have been troubled because, as we will see in Chapter 4, insider dealing has been even commoner in Tokyo than in London. (Indeed, one of the attractions to foreigners of setting up operations in Tokyo was the chance it gave of becoming an insider.) The most important part of the London securities markets, in Eurobonds, actually has partial exemption from the insider dealing controls in the Financial Services Act.[84]

The campaign against insider trading is thus rather more than a functional response by the British state to the changing structure of world markets. In part it represents a direct transmission of the American concerns that we described in Chapter 2. Many of the most important accusations in the Guinness affair, for instance, were prompted by the so-called 'confessions' of the disgraced financier Ivan Boesky. More important still, the American authorities have extended their concerns with insider trading into the international sphere: in November 1986, even in advance of the implementation of the Financial Services Act, the Department of Trade and Industry had concluded a Memorandum of Understanding with the Securities and Exchange Commission and the Commodity Futures Trading Commission, covering the exchange of information relating to insider trading and other forms of market manipulation.[85]

The transmission of American concerns reinforced the effect of domestic political processes. From the conclusion of the Goodison/Parkinson agreement of July 1983 the state was deeply and publicly involved in the reconstruction of financial markets, principally with the object of preserving London's leading position in a world marked by competitive struggles between rival centres. This involvement was, we have seen, the culmination of a slow change in the state's roles and capacities that had already been occurring for several decades. The rise of the state was accelerated because, by the 1980s, it was clear that reforming coalitions within the City could not, unassisted, defeat the traditional interests who were doing well out of restrictive practices. It took state intervention to destroy the old guard. This act of state intervention had consequences similar to those witnessed in the American case. After 1983, City regulation became increasingly politicised. The Praetorian Guard in the Bank of England that had once defended the City elite from democratic politics was no longer a reliable protector – as its desertion in 1982 showed. Mr Parkinson's announcement of his agreement with Goodison produced a hail of abuse in Parliament and the media. The Secretary of State was accused of fixing a deal to suit the Conservative Party's traditional friends in the City.[86] The significance of the abuse was that it signalled the growing politicisation of financial regulation. For the next three-and-a-half years, as the Financial Services Act was first prepared, and then carried through Parliament, the City's affairs were in the centre of the political process – in Whitehall lobbying, in the adversarial party struggle at Westminster and near the top of the media's investigative activities. The height of the campaign against City 'fraud' and insider dealing, in 1985–86, also coincided with the peak of the arguments about the Financial Services Bill.

The politicisation that followed state intervention helps explain why scandal in financial markets claimed so much attention after 1983, but even this does not fully explain why insider dealing in particular should have been the special focus of attention. To account for this we have to recall a feature that was important in the American case: the issue attention process in democratic politics. For a brief period in 1985–86 it seemed that the more general problem of financial fraud would claim most attention. Yet while fraud remains a serious concern among regulators it has never quite achieved the prominence given to insider dealing. This is because financial fraud is too complex to provide the material for journalistic exposes or partisan abuse. The complexity of financial fraud has, indeed, been a major obstacle to detection, prosecution and conviction: juries of lay people, for instance, have often been completely baffled by the technicalities of some fraud cases. The problem is so great that the government's own Committee on Fraud Trials recommended the abolition of trial by jury in complex fraud cases.[87] By contrast, insider dealing is a comparatively straightforward offence which can nevertheless generate a high moral charge. By contrast with fraud cases, which often take years to bring to court, it can also lead to quick and dramatic conclusions: the detection, exposure, stigmatisation and conviction of Geoffrey Collier all took place within a few months (November 1986 to July 1987).

When we bear in mind these general considerations, the particular shape of events in Britain after 1985 becomes readily explicable. The Conservative Government was faced with a Parliamentary opposition anxious to capitalise on City scandals. The Conservatives' closeness to City interests could obviously be electorally damaging. The Thatcher Administration, in the middle of its ambitious privatisation schemes, also had a clear interest in convincing small investors that trading rules in the City markets were honest and fair. Thus the longer term changes in the politics of financial regulation, and the more immediate calculations of the Conservative government, combined to create the campaign against insider trading.

The regulation of insider dealing in the United Kingdom and the United States shows many common features. This is due in part to the transmission of American influences across the Atlantic, and in part to the fact that similar pressures shape financial regulation in the two countries. The growth of state intervention politicised regulation on both sides of the Atlantic. Insider dealing was an activity ideally suited to the attention process of the social actors characteristic of pluralistic democracy, such as politicians and investigative journalists. The campaign against insider trading has been fiercer in the United States than in the United Kingdom because in Britain the exposure of the financial elite to politics has been less complete. Backbench MPs in the Commons command nothing like the attention and resources available to Congress; investigative journalism in Britain is less highly developed than in the United States. In addition, the Thatcher Government has enjoyed one stroke of good fortune: no prominent Conservative has yet been implicated in an insider dealing scandal. When we turn to Japan we will discover that the exposure of insider trading not only destroys financial reputations; when politicians are implicated the results can be disastrous for individual careers and for the stability of an administration. But before examining Japan we need to draw together the strands of the British case.

6 CONCLUSION: CRISIS, DECLINE AND MESO-CORPORATISM

The history of the financial services revolution in Britain during the 1980s resembles in important respects the recent history of other parts of the British economy. It is a tale of decline. London's original preeminence as an international financial centre rested on Britain's world preeminence in the last century. Sterling was the major world currency, Britain was the regulator of the international financial system and British banks were major world financial institutions. This preeminence was already passing away before 1914; the Great War and the Great Depression completed the process. When London re-emerged in the 1950s as a great world centre it did so in a very different way. London's new prominence rested neither on the strength of the British economy, nor on the competitive capacities of British firms. It was, instead, largely a regulatory creation: the informal and consensual regulatory style practised by the Bank of England made London attractive to the emerging 'Euromarkets', especially to American institutions trying to escape a complex home regulatory system. The domestic British financial system – especially the most important part located in the City – meanwhile continued to work through the meso-corporatism evolved after the First World War. Even before the financial services revolution of the 1980s meso-corporatism was under pressure from the twin forces of capitalism and pluralist democracy. The meso-corporatist institutions simply could not suppress competitive struggles, nor the new interests created by these struggles: these are the lessons of the history of take-over regulation, and the slow growth of a more codified, institutionalised and juridified system which that history illustrates. The abolition of exchange controls in 1979 further exposed domestic institutions to wider world competition: and the abolition of controls in Britain was itself only part of a more general movement towards the international integration of markets and the organisation of competitive struggles on a global scale. Yet at the end of the decade the Stock Exchange – the institution crucial to breaking the log-jam obstructing reform – was itself internally deadlocked between reformers and opponents of change.

The wider political system had, however, now created new conditions. There existed an alternative ideology, embodied in restrictive practices legislation, capable of challenging one of the key assumptions of the ideology of self-regulation: the assumption that the markets had the right to organise competitive practices independent of public control. The ideology embodied in restrictive practices legislation said, by contrast, that the state had the right to intervene in markets in order to ensure free and fair competition. In the Office of Fair Trading this ideology had a powerful institutional advocate, led by a shrewd and well connected Director General who was adept at using the media for the Office's campaigns. By the beginning of the 1980s the London Stock Exchange, having exhausted its pleas to successive ministers, was in a similar position to that occupied by the New York Stock Exchange a decade earlier: it had to find, for the Restrictive Practices Court, an intellectu- ally coherent defence of arrangements that had once been unthinkingly sanctioned by the power of a hegemonic ideology of self-regulation. Not even the 'conservatives' inside the Exchange were sure that this was possible.[88]

The slow and expensive progress to the Court hearings was publicly stopped by the Goodison/Parkinson agreement, but was in effect halted in 1982 when the Bank of England deserted to the side of the reformers. This act of desertion was, in narrative terms, perhaps the decisive moment in the genesis of the financial services revolution. The Bank's desertion, however, was itself due to wider political changes. Once a City institution, the Bank was now a state institution. As a state institution it had its own interests to defend – both in Whitehall and in the international community of financial regulators. Its standing in both was tied to Lon- don's continuing prominence as a financial centre – which, we have already seen, was distinct from the international success of native British firms. By comparison with the need to secure London's international position, the interests of the section of British capitalism represented by the more backward parts of the stockbroking community were of minor importance.

At the beginning of the 1980s the competitive struggles between finan- cial centres intensified, as the organisation of financial markets took on an increasingly global nature. By the start of the decade a marked shift in the centre of financial gravity was noticeable. The Japanese financial markets and Japanese financial institutions emerged to challenge the post-war American domination. Tokyo became a major arena in the financial services revolution. In London and New York the twin forces of capitalism and democracy had exercised decisive influences over meso-corporatist regulation. Japan was formally capitalist and formally democratic. Yet by Anglo-American standards Japanese capitalism was a peculiar kind of capitalism; and pluralist democracy in Japan was a recent, and perhaps not deeply rooted, American transplant. In these conditions could meso-corporatist regulation exist? And if it existed, what would happen to it in the face of world markets dominated by struggles for competitive advantage?

We will try to answer these questions in Chapter 4.[89]

4 Japan: Meso-corporatism and Industrial Power

> Without protection by some non-bourgeois group, the bourgeoisie is politically helpless and unable not only to lead its nation but even to take care of its particular class interests. Which amounts to saying that it needs a master.

1 INTRODUCTION

Japanese institutions are now central to the world financial services revolution. The most obvious signs of this centrality are the sheer size of Japanese financial services firms and their astonishing success in world markets in the 1980s. Japanese banks dominate the standard rankings of the world's largest banks. Japanese institutions now have a larger market share than do their American rivals in London, the world's leading international banking centre outside Japan. Three of the five top underwriters in the Eurobond market in 1987 were Japanese (Nomura, Daiwa and Yamaichi).[1] By most measures of stock value Tokyo is the world's leading stock exchange. During the 1980s Japan emerged as the world's leading creditor nation, playing a central role in funding the American Federal deficit.

In brief, the biggest banks, securities firms, insurance companies, stock exchanges and lenders are all Japanese. On these grounds alone Japan is due a place in any analysis of the financial services revolution. But the relevance of the Japanese experience is more pointed still. As the 1980s wore on, the success of Japanese firms in world markets, and the potential riches awaiting foreign firms who could break into Japanese markets, became the most important influences in the world financial services revolution.

Japan's importance in world financial services industries is due to the best known fact about that country: for nearly four decades she has been the most successful of all capitalist economies. Any understanding of the politics of the financial services revolution in Japan therefore has to begin with the debate about the wider politics of the Japanese economic miracle. This debate has focused chiefly on the state's contribution to that miracle. Until recently, the image of the Japanese state as both 'smart' and 'strong' powerfully influenced attempts to understand the governmental origins of the economic success.[2] The image is expressed in popular form by the notion of 'Japan Incorporated', where the bureaucracy – or even a single Ministry like MITI – is pictured as the corporate board shrewdly directing a unified economy. Thus:

> The Japanese government corresponds to corporate headquarters, responsible for planning and coordination, formation of long-term policies and major investment decisions. The large corporations of Japan are akin to corporate divisions.[3]

This is a popularisation of scholarly descriptions that stress the role of the bureaucratic elite in managing both Japanese domestic markets and Japanese intervention in international trade. The most influential of these accounts is Johnson's study of the Ministry of International Trade and Industry. Johnson argues that a range of contingent factors – late development, a large population, the need to trade, and the constraints of the balance of payments – have turned Japan into a 'developmental state' where 'economic interests are explicitly subordinated to political objectives . . . . For more than 50 years the Japanese state has given its first priority to economic development'.[4]

The view that the Japanese state is the engineer of economic change typically points to three instruments at its disposal. The first is a powerful bureaucracy, typified by MITI, the subject of Johnson's study. The second is the device of 'administrative guidance', by which 'guidance' akin to compulsion is issued by bureaucrats and accepted by firms.[5] The discretionary character of the system of administrative guidance is commonly held to confer a special ability flexibly to respond to changing economic circumstances.[6] Third, Zsyman and others have argued that the character of the financial system offers a powerful instrument in the management of industrial change: bank domination of the system of credit allocation, coupled with state control over the banking system, are thought to ensure industrial restructuring in the face of economic change.[7]

The notion that Japan is a society possessed of superior political mechanisms for organising its economy in the struggle for advantage in world markets has influenced not only general accounts of the country's economic miracle; it has also shaped accounts of the most recent phases of the financial services revolution. It is indeed tempting to picture the rise to world eminence of Japanese financial institutions as part of a strategic exercise by which the controllers of the Japanese economy have targeted successive sectors of world markets. 'Japanese banks are beginning to export cash in much the same way as Toyota exported cars', say Wright and Pauli: 'just as termites are blind but still able to work diligently towards a common goal, the Japanese financial services houses are all driving towards the same target – domination of markets.'[8] Spindler puts the point more soberly, but still sees a strong, independent state as the key actor in financial politics: 'The Japanese government has regularly operated both as a major force above Japanese financial markets (the supervisor) and as a force in those markets (the coordinator and intermediary).'[9]

The 'developmental state' model, and its popular relative 'Japan Incorporated', deeply influenced initial attempts to understand the significance of the modern Japanese state.[10] But more recent observations have compelled a qualification of this account. Four sceptical observations are noteworthy. The first examines the significance of divisions within the bureaucracy. Johnson's monumental study of MITI by no means ignored bureaucratic divisions. On the contrary, he suggested that 'internal bureaucratic disputes, factional infighting and conflict among ministries' were central to the process of policy change precisely because so much depended on the guidance of a ministerial structure.[11] Yet the accumulation of case studies of such in-fighting, coupled with an apparent decline in MITI's supremacy over other agencies, has thrown into question prevailing images of strategic coherence.[12]

A second source of difficulty concerns the significance of 'administrative guidance', the importance of which is universally recognised, but the foundations of which are disputed. Does it represent the domination of the state over private interests, or is it a reflection of a different sort of public/private partnership? Young, for instance, argues that the content of guidance is usually the result of extensive consultations with affected interests, and that this consultation is a necessary condition of effectiveness: 'the interactive consultation process that precedes the issuance of guidance is a significant and necessary step for the effective accomplishment of administrative goals and objectives.'[13]

Uncertainty about the significance of administrative guidance is connected to a third issue, one which lies at the heart of the events examined in this chapter. It concerns the balance of power between the state and business. The most vigorous rejection of the 'strong state' model of Japan has been offered by Samuels in his study of energy policy. 'Most available descriptions of the Japanese political economy', he writes, 'exaggerate state power at the expense of private power.' The reality is that policy is the product of 'reciprocal consent . . . the mutual accommodation of state and market.' This accommodation has been forced on the state 'because in the development of Japanese commerce and industry powerful and stable private actors emerged who established enduring alliances with politicians and bureaucrats'.[14]

Differences about the extent of bureaucratic unity, about the foundations of administrative guidance and about the links between the state and private interests are all connected to a fourth area of doubt, concerning the character and source of consensus in the Japanese system. The idea that there is an identifiable unitary purpose driving Japan links the crudest 'Japan Incorporated' and the most sophisticated 'developmental state' model. Muramatsu and Krauss, however, while accepting in some degree the 'strong state' characterisation, picture consensus as the short-lived result of a political strategy pursued by conservative political forces. Consensus did not result from a 'mystical cultural process . . . For much of the post-war period, there was not even a consensus among the conservative elite, much less a national consensus . . . rather than economic growth being the consequence of an existing consensus, the national consensus that did emerge was probably more the result of the [conservative] policy line's effectiveness as a political strategy for attaining political stability and economic growth. That consensus was also to be short-lived'.[15]

This brief review shows that there presently exists no uncontested model of the Japanese state's economic role on which we might draw to make sense of the financial services revolution in Tokyo. The unity of the Japanese state, the nature and efficacy of the regulatory instruments at its disposal, the extent of its autonomy from private interests, the character of the consensus underpinning its policies: all are the subject of dispute.

The continuing debate is, however, focused on identifying the nature of Japanese uniqueness, for the very good reason that the policy performance of the Japanese state has itself been unique. It has been natural to search for what was special in the Japanese case, since the results of Japanese economic management in the post-war years have been outstandingly different from the results achieved elsewhere.

Given the unique quality of policy outcomes it would be astonishing not to discover unique features in the connections linking the Japanese state to the economy; and in the regulation of financial services it is therefore not at all surprising to discover some Japanese arrangements very different from those in the United Kingdom and the United States. The truly surprising feature of the Japanese case, however, is not the peculiarities that emerge in the succeeding pages; it is the degree to which there are continuities with the Anglo-American systems in institutional patterns and policy outcomes. Two of these emerge strikingly in the succeeding pages. The first is the markedly visible bias to meso-corporatism in regulation. Japan has its own individual institutional structure, and the way that structure works is mediated by national cultural traits. The strength and depth of meso-corporatist arrangements are nevertheless remarkable. The power of ideologies of business self-regulation; the extent to which regulatory tasks are done by private interests; the way restrictions on competition have been entwined with those regulatory tasks: to a remarkable degree these resemble features encountered in the United States and the United Kingdom.

The second similarity is more striking still. Scandal and competitive struggle turned out to be the twin agencies of regulatory crisis in the United Kingdom and the United States. Not only do these two agents reappear in the Japanese case; they are driving meso-corporatist regulation in the same directions as that taken by the Anglo-American systems. The reasons, to anticipate, are two-fold. First, struggles for competitive advantage in markets have destabilised the hierarchies of interests organised under meso-corporatism, just as happened in the Anglo-American systems. Second, Japanese firms in the 1980s operated in a system of world markets. The most striking feature of these markets in the decade was, we shall see, the extent to which Japanese institutions challenged the once supreme Americans. This challenge, and the American response, holds the most important clue to events in Tokyo during the decade. To put the point starkly: there is indeed a key state actor in the Japanese financial services revolution, but it is the American rather than the Japanese state.

The remainder of the chapter is developed in a manner similar to the case studies of the United States and the United Kingdom: a sketch of the institutional structure of regulation, an account of historical origins and evolution, an examination of the forces producing regulatory change and an account of the growth of insider trading regulation.

2   THE INSTITUTIONS OF MESO-CORPORATISM

The organisation of financial services regulation in the United States and the United Kingdom is in one striking way remarkably similar: regulatory tasks are dispersed through a wide range of private, quasi-private and free-standing public agencies. The Japanese structure looks, at first glance, very different. Its distinctiveness originated partly in the arrangements created during the immediate post-war years. These arrangements involved state regulation of price competition and market entry, with the object of creating a financial structure where a small number of institutions provided cheap capital for selected industrial sectors. In Eccleston's words:

At the macro level the state in Japan has managed the financial markets by controlling the links between savers and investors in a fragmented and specialised structure. City banks are encouraged to over-lend to maintain the expansion of industry . . . [the] banks gain the prestige of being associated with leading national firms and the advantage of paying lower rates for Central Bank support. The state has an immensely powerful lever for its priorities in industrial investment, which it supplements with inter-agency personnel transfers especially of early-retiring officials.[16]

The distinctiveness of a state-marshalled financial system is reinforced by the way financial regulation is organised within the state structure. One institution stands supreme, and that institution, the Ministry of Finance (MOF) is a central department of state headed by a Cabinet Minister. The Ministry unites regulatory functions which in the United States and the United Kingdom are shared by a mixture of private and public bodies: it licenses and supervises banks; in the post-war era of regulated interest rates it has been the chief controller of the level at which rates are set; it licenses and supervises firms in the securities industry; it fixes rules governing the issue and sale of securities; as the country's Treasury ministry it is responsible for the formulation of fiscal policy, and thus also for managing public debt; and it is the chief institution responsible for international financial relations, including the management of balance of payments and foreign exchange policy.[17] The Ministry is a key part of the legendary Japanese bureaucracy; indeed in recent years it has rivalled the prestige and influence of even the famed Ministry of International Trade and Industry.[18] The MOF, like other important Japanese Ministries, is led by a powerful and able bureaucracy, selected on graduation from an elite university (overwhelmingly Tokyo).[19]

The unusual (by Anglo-American standards) concentration of functions in the Ministry of Finance, and the domination of that Ministry by a small, socially cohesive bureaucracy seem to suggest that, in financial services at least, the Japanese state does have an institution capable of shaping policy according to strategically coherent aims. The Ministry is undoubtedly the key institution in the system; but in reality its grasp over the making and implementation of policy is limited, and its own importance is due as much to the way it is a cockpit within which conflicting interests battle, as to any capacity to act as the authoritative controller of Japanese financial markets.

The most obvious limit to the scope of the Ministry's jurisdiction lies in the fact that it operates as part of a wider complex of public institutions, whose relations are governed by a shifting and contested division of labour over the making and execution of policy. The most striking illustration of this is provided by the MOF's relationship with the Ministry of Posts and Telecommunications (MPT). The MPT, through its management of the country's Post Offices, is both a major player with interests to defend in the Japanese financial market place, and a major player with jurisdictional interests to defend in Japanese regulatory politics. The nation's 20 000 Post Offices are the most important part of the domestic retail banking system. Their importance is closely connected to the distribution of regulatory authority – for instance, to the tax concessions on the interest from Post Office accounts that gave the Post Office a considerable competitive advantage against the rest of the banking system. The Post Office's success in the marketplace has also created a powerful political interest group, in the shape of the nation's postmasters, who are an important organisational and electoral influence in the ruling Liberal Democratic Party.[20] As we shall see in Section 4 of this chapter, attempts in the 1980s by the Ministry of Finance to introduce competitive changes have been resisted by the MPT, acting in defence of both its regulatory jurisdiction and of the interests that it sponsors.

A second important limit to the scope of the Ministry of Finance's jurisdiction over financial services arises from the way the regulatory system attributes public functions to 'private' institutions. The most striking instances of this are provided by the securities industry. The stock exchanges (there are eight, of which Tokyo and Osaka are by the far the largest) were in the past private institutions operating under a 'franchise' granted by the state.[21] During the post-war occupation they were reorganised under American influence: the constitution of the Tokyo Exchange, for instance, is modelled on that of the San Francisco Stock Exchange. Under the 1948 Securities Transaction Law the Exchanges are licensed by the Ministry of Finance, but are self-governing institutions choosing their own ruling body and – as we shall notice in the case of insider dealing – exercising considerable control over their own trading practices.[22] Although the Ministry of Finance has the power to enforce rules on the Exchanges 'no case has been reported thus far where the Finance Ministry has taken enforcement action against a stock exchange'.[23] This delegation of regulatory authority stretches to surveillance of market practices, which is largely in the hands of the Exchanges.

This attribution of regulatory status to 'private' institutions is not confined to the Exchanges. It is also a feature of important trade associations in financial services. The Japanese Securities Dealers' Association, for example, is by no means simply an independent pressure group: its membership encompasses all securities firms, and it exercises regulatory authority over those firms. It has a particularly significant role in the regulation of the important over-the-counter market in securities. The Association is registered with the Ministry of Finance as a 'self-regulatory' body; its institutional relationship to the Ministry resembles that between the MOF and the Stock Exchanges.[24] Similar arrangements hold in the investment trust industry, a major segment of the financial services sector. Regulation here is carried out through the Securities Investment Trust Association, whose rules are subject to MOF approval.[25] The single most important reason for this delegation is that the MOF is a small Ministry, quite unequipped to carry out the executive tasks of detailed surveillance and rule enforcement. The Securities Bureau, for instance, had in 1988 an investigative staff of only 140; the comparable figures for the American SEC was 600.[26] These formal arrangements for harnessing trade associations to the regulatory tasks are matched by more general features of the organisation of capital markets. The most distinctive feature of the Japanese system in the post-war years has been the extent to which a network of banks, some private, some semi-public, benefited from publicly enforced restrictive practices in return for channelling investment finance to selected industries. As a reward for carrying out the public policy of providing cheap capital, banks enjoyed extensive protection, until the later 1980s, from domestic competitive struggles. As Wathen summarised the arrangements: 'Two features dominated, namely regulated interest rates and strict compartmentalisation between institutions . . . The main consideration in the formulation of Japan's financial system was to engineer an economic recovery, financial markets being a conduit for this rather than a growth sector in their own right.'[27]

Formal institutional arrangements, suggesting as they do an extensive attribution of regulatory tasks to private and semi-private institutions, are reflected also in the actual patterns of policy making and implementation. In the securities industry the Securities Dealers' Association is dominated by the four biggest firms (Nomura, Daiwa, Nikko, Yamaichi) who between them account for 40 per cent of the business in the securities markets. There exists a symbiotic relationship between the 'Big Four' and the Securities Bureau of the Ministry of Finance. An informal club of vice-presidents of the biggest firms meets regularly, and those meetings are attended by officials of the Securities Bureau of the MOF. This close relationship stretches to the management of markets. The response to the world-wide stock market crash in 1987 is an instructive example: several authoritative sources say, independently, that the Big Four entered the market, at the prompting of the Ministry of Finance, in order to support prices in

Tokyo.[28] This cooperation is particularly noticeable in the Bond Market. The standing Conference on Government Bond Issuance and the Bond Flotation Council, for instance, link representatives of public bodies (the Ministry of Finance, the Central Bank) with firms in the underwriting syndicate, to discuss the organisation of bond issues.[29] This arrangement reflects an extended post-war history of market management by institutions uniting public and private representatives, stretching back to the Bond Issuance Adjustment Council established in 1947.[30] The arrangement also reflects a more general Japanese preference, favouring the attachment to ministries of 'large numbers of advisory committees . . . made up of representatives from business and the academic community'.[31] Thus the Financial Problems Study Group, originally established in 1977 by the Banking Bureau of the MOF, has been a key forum bringing together competing interests for over a decade in discussions of reform options.[32] The fusion of public and private roles is encouraged by the Japanese practice (quaintly translated as 'descent from Heaven'), of early retirement by bureaucrats and their transfer to other posts, frequently in the private sector: 'in 1980, for every five career officers in the MOF, there was one retired officer in a financial institution.'[33]

The Ministry of Finance is the pivot around which the Japanese system of financial regulation turns; there exists in neither Britain nor in the United States a comparable concentration of functions and influence. But it is the pivot of a system with a marked bias to meso-corporatism. This bias has been reflected in the structure of the financial system: in the organisation of private interests into segmented markets operating significant restrictions on price competition and market entry; in the way those interests play key roles in implementing industrial policy by channelling investment capital to chosen sectors; and in the way the specialised activity of financial regulation is itself done.

We thus now have two qualifications to the image of the Ministry of Finance as the supreme governor of the financial system: it has to work in a governmental structure where its jurisdiction is challenged by other public agencies; and it operates through a system where private firms, trade associations, and formally constituted self-regulatory organisations play key roles in the policy process. To these two observations we must note a third feature of the institutional structure of the MOF: precisely by virtue of its wide range of responsibilities it has incorporated within itself some of the most powerful conflicting interests within the financial markets. Horne's study of the domestic Japanese conflicts over regulatory change in the late 1970s and early 1980s illustrates the way these conflicts have been internalised, and the way they are in turn shaped by the structure of the Ministry. He writes of this period, with respect to the MOF:

> Disagreements between the Banking Bureau and the Securities Bureau were numerous, reflecting their very different jurisdictional interests. The Securities Bureau was concerned primarily with the development and management of direct financing alternatives such as the development of the bonds and equities market. Its day to day contacts were with the securities companies, and hence it was often seen as representing their interests. On the other hand, the Banking Bureau was involved in regulating the banking sector and was largely responsible for policy that related to the banks. A close, although at times uneasy, relationship existed between the Banking Bureau and the banking sector.[34]

The institutional world of Japanese financial services regulation exercises, we shall see, a powerful influence in the policy struggles marking the Japanese financial services revolution. This world consists of a dense network of connections and interests, at the centre of which are the various bureaux of the Ministry of Finance. The structure is the product of many uniquely Japanese influences, but in one key respect the Japanese experience resembles that of Britain and the United States. In the Anglo-American systems regulatory structures and regulatory politics are indelibly marked by past historical crises – by the Great Depression in the American case, and by the Great War in the British. The Japanese system is likewise the product of past crises. To these, and to their consequences, we now turn.

3 ORIGINS AND EVOLUTION OF MESO-CORPORATISM

The crises that created the modern Japanese system date back over a century. As in the United States and the United Kingdom, the structure of markets and the structure of regulation have been entwined. Financial markets have deep roots in Japanese economic history: for example, a futures market in rice was organised in Tokyo as early as 1730.[35] The modern system is, however, the result of the Meiji modernisation – that burst of reform in the latter decades of the nineteenth century produced by the impact of foreign power on the Japanese society. Within the space of a decade there were established securities exchanges (Tokyo and Osaka, 1878), a central bank (1882) and a regulatory structure for commercial banking (Bank Act of 1890).[36]

These institutional innovations borrowed from abroad: stock exchange regulation drew on the experience of London; the central bank was modelled on that in Belgium.[37] But this appearance of foreign borrowing concealed distinctive patterns of behaviour. The most important concerned the mobilisation of finance for industrial investment. Gerschenkron has shown that 'late starters' like Japan needed, in the ascent to industrialisation, purposive institutions rapidly to mobilise capital for investment.[38] With poorly developed securities markets, the banks performed the function of providing funds. Tsutsui writes:

> From the beginnings of industrialisation in the Meiji period corporate finance in Japan has been predominantly indirect, that is, firms have tended to raise investment funds from financial intermediaries (especially banks) rather than by obtaining the required capital 'directly' through sale of equities to individual savers.[39]

This pattern was due less to state direction than to the creation of a corporatist partnership between banks and the authorities. Banking regulation was

> informal, extra-legal . . . the monetary authorities did not have the power or inclination to dictate banking policy to the private sector, seeking rather to advise, encourage and otherwise work obliquely to attain their aims . . . what was most striking about public-private financial relations during the first 50 years of modern banking in Japan was not so much the extent of official influence as the extent to which a cooperative, constructive atmosphere surrounded dealings between the government and commercial banking.[40]

This institutional structure was subsequently reshaped by three further crises. The first was a great banking collapse in 1927, the product of intense competitive struggles that led to a wave of failures. The result was the Banking Law of 1928 which prohibited banks from engaging in non-banking activities and gave the Ministry of Finance power to license firms. This legislation was not superseded until the banking reforms of 1981.[41] The second crisis was associated with the rise of militarism and the war economy. Militarism did not alter the basic character of the financial system – domination by a small number of banking institutions acting as channels of industrial finance. But the era of militarism and war produced significant structural and regulatory developments: the growing domination of the banking system by a small number of institutions; the consolidation of the 'Zaibatsu' system, a uniquely Japanese form of finance capitalism involving strategic control over networks of industrial firms by a small number of powerful banks; and growth in the influence of state agencies over the financial system.[42] The last development included, most notably, the reorganisation in 1942 of the central bank along the lines of the German Reichsbank; this reform still shapes the power and the role of the Japanese central bank.[43] The Ministry of Finance, which had been a significant regulatory actor since the mid-1920s, also consolidated its position and laid foundations for its post-war importance.

The third crisis posed unprecedented problems for the financial structure. Military defeat in 1945 left currency and banking in chaos; led to nearly seven years of American occupation; and changed the wider political environment of financial markets by substituting a system of nominally competitive democratic politics for the preceding dictatorial arrangements. The period is notable for the attempt by some of the occupation authorities to remake both the financial structure and financial regulation on an American model – and is notable also for the failure of most of these efforts. There were three notable components to the reform measures. The first was the attempt to break up the biggest banks that controlled the Zaibatsu system, an attempt legitimised by American ideologies of anti-trust and by the claim that the Zaibatsu were partly responsible for the Japanese state's military aggression.[44] The second, related, component was the effort to reorganise the securities industry along the lines of the reforms introduced in the United States in the 1930s. The securities law of 1947 (operative 1948) transformed the stock exchanges from private companies into institutions governed, as in the American system, by their members; and, in Article 65 of that legislation, replicated the provisions of the US Glass-Steagall Act which prohibited banks from offering or underwriting most classes of securities.[45] Finally, during the occupation period an attempt was made to match the reorganisation of markets along American lines with corresponding changes in the institutional structure of the system of regulation. Changes in the constitution of the central bank were designed to make it more independent of the central machinery of the state, in the manner of the Federal Reserve; while the securities legislation of 1948 established a Securities Exchanges Commission, a three-member group of independent commissioners supported by a staff of over 140, whose functions and powers were in some degree modelled on the American Securities and Exchange Commission.[46]

With one significant exception these efforts to 'Americanise' the financial structure failed. Observers as different in their accounts as Adams,

Hadley and Tsutsui agree that the attempt to break the power of the biggest banks at the heart of the pre-war Zaibatsu system did not succeed. 'The banks', writes Hadley, 'came through the wringer of the deconcentration programme virtually intact.'[47] Tsutsui, while arguing that the bank-coordinated Keiretsu that emerged after the war were not as rigid as the old Zaibatsu system, still concludes that: 'the Occupation presided over the rehabilitation of Japan's wartime financial arrangements, never directly challenging the government controls, legal controversies or tendencies in corporate finance and structural evolution which derived from the years of militarism.'[48] (Keiretsu are the post-war descendants of Zaibatsu – clusters of firms gathered into alliances controlled and co-ordinated through financial institutions.)

Not only was the post-war economic miracle founded on a bank-dominated financial system; the end of the occupation was marked by the revival – for instance in the foreign exchange market – of the institution of 'special' banks endowed by the state with market privileges in return for performing special tasks. The efforts at reform of the regulatory structure were similarly unsuccessful. The Bank of Japan, far from acquiring the independence of the Federal Reserve, remained a junior partner, though an important partner, of the Ministry of Finance. The attempt to create a Japanese SEC likewise came to nothing: in August 1951, as the Occupation drew to its close, the Commission was absorbed into the Ministry of Finance. In its place was created an Advisory Committee with no power.[49]

Of the efforts at reform under the Occupation only one left an enduring mark: article 65 of the Securities and Exchange Law, by keeping the banks out of the business of issuing and underwriting most classes of securities, created space for the growth of the securities companies. By the 1980s, as we shall shortly see, article 65 was one of the most hotly contested issues between the interests doing battle over the terms of regulatory reform in Tokyo.

The exact causes of this failure to 'Americanise' the Japanese system are the subject of debate, but the broad argument is well established. There was no coherent plan of reconstruction because the Occupiers were themselves divided over how far the competitive course suggested by anti-trust ideology should be pursued. American priorities soon shifted from reform to the conciliation of domestic elites and the integration of Japan into the Western alliance, thus weakening further the arguments of those who wished to impose Americanisation on the financial system. With the end of the occupation there occurred a reassertion of control by traditional administrative and economic elites. This resulted in the abolition of innovations like the American-style Securities Exchanges Commission, and the recreation of a corporatised banking structure.

The significance of the occupation 'crisis' is that it established the Japanese institutional pattern for the crucial succeeding decades covering the country's rise to a position of world economic preeminence: 'The institutional structure of the Japanese financial system was much the same in 1980 as it was in 1955.'[50]

This sketch may suggest that, despite the great caesura of 1945–52, the financial services industry in Japan has, in the post-war years, been characterised by a process of regressive evolution to a traditional Japanese pattern. But beneath the enduring institutional forms, competitive struggles and structural changes were, even before the major struggles of the 1980s, altering the character of the system. Three particular changes are noteworthy because they anticipated much that was to be important throughout the 1980s.

First, although the strict segmentation of markets and strict suppression of price (interest rate) competition were cardinal principles of financial regulation, competitive struggles nevertheless continued and, by their structural consequences, altered the balance of interests in markets. The simplicities of a state-sponsored, bank-dominated financial structure that had emerged in the post-war era of capital shortage gave way to more complex patterns as economic success generated corporate profits that could be used for investment, and as rising levels of real income swelled the volume of personal savings. In the early 1970s, with securities markets still comparatively underdeveloped, private savings became one of the major objects of competitive struggle. One of the chief agents in the struggle was a state institution, the Post Office. Historically, Post Office deposits carrying low rates of interest had been a major means of raising investment finance cheaply. But in the 1970s, in the struggle for a share of the growing pool of Japanese savings, the Post Office became a source of innovation in the financial system. By virtue of its position in the state machinery, the interest it offered on deposits was tax free – in effect conferring on the Post Office a major price advantage in struggles with other institutions. The advance of the Post Office in the market for deposits was remarkable: it had under 40 per cent of individual deposits in 1965, and over 64% a decade later.[51] This powerful institutional interest, when coupled with the interests savers had in tax evasion, was to prove a major feature of the struggles for regulatory change in the 1980s.

Competitive struggles and structural change were connected to the second important evolutionary development that was happening even before the world financial services revolution burst upon the Japanese markets: there took place an incremental, but still significant, codification and juridification of the regulatory system. Thus a new banking law of 1981, the first significant change in that part of the regulatory system since 1927, incorporated into statute much that had previously enjoyed the status of 'administrative guidance'.[52] A more striking instance still was provided by the securities industry, where in the 1960s competitive struggles led to collapses of firms. The crisis began in 1964 as a result of imprudent commitments induced by intense competition. The result was legislation to introduce compulsory licencing of companies, compulsory amalgamation of separate representative associations, the extension of regulatory powers and legal standing to associations, and the reorganisation of the securities bureau inside the Ministry of Finance.[53] Thus, some of the key institutional actors in the regulatory struggles of the 1980s turn out to be the result of a regulatory crisis of two decades previously.

The growth in the breadth and complexity of the interests struggling in financial markets, and the phenomena of codification and juridification, amounted to slow changes. A third alteration was more obviously cata-strophic for the regulatory system. After 1973, in the recession that now succeeded the 'long boom' in the great capitalist economies, the Japanese state experienced a serious fiscal crisis. The simplest measure of this is the growth of government debt. Between 1970 and 1980 the nominal value of outstanding government bonds grew more than twenty-fold, while their value as a percentage of all outstanding securities rose from under a tenth to over a third.[54] The interest on debt, which before 1975 had been around 1 per cent of Gross National Product, had by the early years of the next decade grown to 4 per cent.[55]

These statistics are a crude sign of a momentous historical shift. The fiscal crisis had driven the state to the securities markets to fund its debt. The organisation of bond issues and underwriting was quintessentially corporatist: that is, private firms fulfilled their roles in cooperation with the state, in return for privileges like a guaranteed part of the bond issue. Before 1975, 'the purchase of the bonds was obligatory . . . Syndicate members, considered to be bound by patriotism, were required to buy the bonds regardless of their below market interest rates'. But the state's appetite for debt after the mid-1970s put these arrangements under intolerable stress. Indeed by the early 1980s the syndicate had refused on a number of occasions to underwrite the bond issue.[56] The price of continuing partnership was a major change in competitive conditions. Between the mid-1970s and the end of the decade there was a gradual relaxation of restrictions on price competition and on restrictions to innovation in the bond and the short-term money markets. The principal object of these relaxations was to create an active secondary market in government debt.[57]

By the end of the 1970s the Japanese state was far from being the kind of omniscient ruler of financial markets hinted at in the imagery of 'Japan Incorporated'. Competitive struggle and structural change were combining to produce incremental codification and juridification of the regulatory system; some state institutions were trying to control competition while others, like the Post Office, were themselves active competitors in markets; and the fiscal crisis was putting immense stress on the partnership between state institutions and private interests in key financial markets. These influences remained observable in the 1980s, but the pace of change was quickened by another factor: the internationalisation of the Japanese markets. With internationalisation Japan became central to the most important part of the financial services revolution: the struggle for competitive advantage in world markets between coalitions of private firms and state agencies. The way this has shaped the regulation of Japanese markets is the theme of the next section.

4   MESO-CORPORATISM AND STRUCTURAL CHANGE

The 1980s were years of extraordinary change in the competitive rules governing Japanese financial markets. By the end of the decade these changes, far from abating, showed every sign of accelerating. Their nature and scope may best be summarised under three headings: the rules governing price competition; the rules governing financial innovation; and the rules governing the entry of firms (either Japanese or foreign) into particular markets. The centrepiece of change in price competition concerns interest rates. The first serious breach in the post-war Japanese restrictive structure happened in 1979 with the introduction of Certificates of Deposit (CDs) in domestic markets. The introduction of Certificates of Deposit (a tradeable instrument issued by a bank to a depositor) had two consequences: it effectively introduced price competition for very large deposits; and, since the markets for different sizes of deposit are not perfectly sealed off from each other, it allowed competitive effects to seep into the markets for smaller deposits. Since the mid-1980s the restrictions on CDs have been progressively eased, and banks have been inventing and marketing a variety of Money Market Certificates (MMCs) designed to allow even comparatively small deposits access to competitive interest rates.[58] Progress nevertheless remained slow: even at the end of 1987 interest rates on 75 per cent of all time deposits in banks were still controlled.[59] In the next eighteen months, however, change accelerated. In April 1988 a wide range of tax breaks on Post Office deposits were abolished. The reform, by removing a major competitive advantage enjoyed by the Post Office, intensified the struggle between it and the banks for the resources of savers.[60] (It also abolished a major source of tax evasion.) By intensifying the competitive struggle the change has put remaining restrictions under severe pressure, as the banks challenge the remaining Post Office privileges. In the Government bond market, too, there has been progressive easing of restrictions on price competition with the introduction, and slow widening, of an 'auction' system in the bond issue.[61]

The spread of price competition has in part been connected to the development of financial innovation: thus the introduction of both Certificates of Deposit and of Money Market Certificates amounted to a Japanese adaptation of instruments pioneered in the Anglo-American systems. This pattern of copying and adaptation of foreign – chiefly American-originated – innovations has been a general mark of the process of innovation. The major change has taken place since the middle of the 1980s. It has involved the introduction both of new financial instruments and new markets. The former have included the launch in 1985 of a futures contract in government bonds by the Tokyo Stock Exchange; the launch of a stock index futures contract on both Osaka and Tokyo three years later; a wide range of bank-marketed foreign currency based instruments designed to allow savers access to foreign financial markets; and the creation of mortgage-backed tradeable securities.[62] Among the new markets created, the single most important is the Tokyo off-shore banking market, established at the beginning of 1987. An 'off-shore' market is beyond national boundaries in a legal, not a physical, sense; it is a market where many domestic banking restrictions are relaxed. Tokyo's market was established to counter the attractions both of London, and of New York's off-shore banking market. (Within eighteen months it was over six times as large as that in New York.)[63] In November 1987 a domestic market in commercial paper (tradeable debt instruments issued by firms to meet their short-term finance needs) was established and, following the passage of legislation in June 1988, specialist financial futures markets will be operating in Tokyo and Osaka in the early 1990s.[64]

The creation of new instruments and new markets, though important in itself, is also significant because of the extent to which it connects to the third feature of recent financial change in Japan: the erosion of the barriers to market entry, both domestic and foreign. In some respects this is the most significant of all changes, marking as it does the partial destruction of the most important traditional feature of the Japanese system, segregation into distinct markets dominated by specialist institutions. Of a wide range of changes, two are especially significant: the increasing circumvention of the barrier, embodied in article 65 of the original 1948 securities legislation, segregating banking from securities; and the lowering of barriers against the entry of foreign firms into Japanese financial markets.

The erosion of article 65 goes back to developments in the 1970s. The original prohibition did not extend to government securities, a comparatively unimportant exception before the fiscal crises of that decade. But the huge expansion in the size of the government bond market, and the creation of an active secondary market, greatly changed the significance of this exemption. Article 65 remains on the statute book, but it is an increasing anachronism. Among the most important breaches have been the entry of foreign banks into the securities business, the decision to allow banking participation in the commercial paper market, and the integration by Japanese firms abroad of their banking and securities arms. These moves have partly been forced on banks by wider structural changes. The long-term credit banks, for example, who for so long formed the centrepiece of the Japanese structure of industrial investment, have been obliged to look to equity markets because their former role has been partly supplanted by securities markets or by internally generated corporate funds.[65]

The lowering of barriers to entry by foreign firms into Japanese markets takes us, as we shall shortly discover, near the heart of the forces creating change in Japan. Two developments are especially important. The first is in the issue market in 10-year government bonds which, because of their sheer volume, 'have become the central instrument for the investment strategy of foreign financial institutions operating in Japan'. The size of the allocation given to foreign firms in the underwriting syndicate was raised in April 1987 and the conditions for foreign participation relaxed.[66] A second key change governs foreign entry to stock markets: at the end of the same year twelve extra seats were allotted on the Tokyo Stock Exchange to foreign firms, bringing the number of foreign members by that date to 22 out of 114.[67]

The significance that can be read into these changes depends on whether the judgement is framed by reference to other financial centres or to past Japanese arrangements. Tokyo is still the most tightly regulated of the world's great financial capitals. There remain powerful barriers to both price competition and to market entry. The limited concessions to foreign participation in the key government bond market, squeezed grudgingly out of the Japanese authorities, are a remarkable contrast to the ease with which Japanese institutions have established themselves in British and

American markets. Domestically there still exist numerous restrictions – notably limits to price competition in securities brokerage, the abolition of which was a key to change in both the United Kingdom and in the United States.

The extent of regulatory change in Japan is therefore, by Anglo-American standards, quite limited. By Japanese standards, however, the phrase 'financial services revolution' is for once not hyperbole. The extent to which interest rate controls have been abolished; the import of exotic foreign financial instruments; the invasion by domestic financial services firms of each other's markets; and the evidence that change is accelerating with the passage of time: all these suggest that the Japanese system is undergoing revolution.

Faced with these changes it is tempting to picture the process in the simple language of deregulation – in other words, as a retreat by the state in the face of competition and innovation in the markets. It is indeed perfectly plain that, in Japan as elsewhere, there have occurred 'repeating cycles of market pressure, innovation and deregulation'.[68] In the Japanese case the most powerful domestic forces have included the state's need to induce markets to funds its debt, and the search by individual savers for rates of return above those offered by the regulated institutions. The power of competitive forces was greatly strengthened by the liberalisation of foreign exchange markets in the Foreign Exchange and Foreign Trade Control Law of 1980.[69] Like the British foreign exchange measure of 1979, it was an acknowledgement of the extent to which financial markets were transcending the boundaries of individual national systems of control. After the reform of the foreign exchange law in 1980 there was, in Feldman's words, a 'flight of domestic borrowers to foreign markets'.[70] There is little doubt that the initially limited easing of restrictions in the late 1970s led to rapid social learning, in which both savers and firms adapted and extended competitive practices in order to undermine or to circumvent remaining controls.

It is worth stressing the significance of competitive struggles in markets because such an emphasis corrects what might be called the 'Japan Incorporated' picture of the financial services revolution.[71] The Japanese state has not been engineering financial change; in critical cases it has been at the mercy of competitive struggles. But this corrective emphasis should not be stressed too much. The Japanese financial services revolution is sometimes a tale of the state's retreat: more commonly, however, it is a story of bargaining and conflict between fractions of the state allied to groups of competing interests inside the industry.

The centrality of state agencies is due to three particularly important considerations. The first is that the circumvention of existing restrictions through financial innovation is not the result of simple opposition between, on the one hand, regulators opposed to change and, on the other, entrepreneurs intent on evading controls; it arises from an elaborately choreographed ritual in which the parties cooperate to test the outer limits of the existing restrictions. The fate of article 65 of the 1948 Law – the article separating banking and securities – is a good example. The Law is suffering a similar fate to the Glass-Steagall legislation in the United States: it is being gradually destroyed both by official redefinitions of what constitutes a security and by the innovations of big firms. There is an alliance, in particular, between officials in the Banking Bureau of the Ministry of Finance and some large banks to test the limits of regulation in this way.[72]

The second reason for the state's centrality is that one state institution, the Post Office, is a major player at the heart of struggles for both regulatory jurisdiction and for market share. The Post Office is usualy described as an opponent of change. In practice, like other important players, its interests are contradictory and its behaviour opportunistic. It has fought a rearguard action against the deregulation of interest rates on small deposits, and against the abolition of tax exemptions on Post Office savings. Yet it has also been a major innovator in retail banking, building its market share substantially in the process.

The themes of contradictory interests and opportunistic behaviour run through the story of the Japanese financial services revolution, and are linked to the third source of state importance. The actors in the markets group and regroup in complex and shifting alliances according to the way particular regulatory issues affect their own complex interests. These shifting alliances in turn encompass agencies of the state. The best documented case is the Ministry of Finance. In the continuing conflicts over the future of Article 65 the Securities Bureau has been allied to securities firms anxious to retain the prohibition on bank entry into their business; the Banking Bureau has been an advocate of reform. In continuing arguments between banks and securities firms over who should be allowed entry to the planned markets in financial futures, the two bureaus also sided with their respective clients and the issue was resolved by a compromise struck within the Ministry.[73]

Even these examples greatly oversimplify the character of conflict, since they suggest that division simply runs downs the line separating banking, securities and their auxiliaries in the state. There also exists, however, significant jurisdictional competition between regulators. In the case of financial futures, for instance, debates about establishing the market were complicated by the competing ambitions of the Tokyo and Osaka Stock Exchanges.[74] The divisions stretch into individual industries and even into firms. The main trade association in the securities industry publicly opposes abolition of article 65 because it keeps banks out of the securities business. But the association is dominated by the Big Four firms, which themselves operate integrated operations abroad.[75]

The state is deeply involved in the Japanese financial services revolution, but it is far from being the arbiter of conflicting interests in the markets; it is fragmented between those tortuous and shifting interests. When we recall in addition the cultural preferences favouring consensus that marks the Japanese bureaucracy, we should perhaps be surprised not by the limited nature of financial change, but by the fact that any change has occurred at all. Indeed the progress of regulatory change has required two critical interventions to break the deadlock between the competing interests. The first we have already encountered. The fiscal crisis of the state after the start of the world recession in 1973 faced regulators with the stark alternative of loosening competitive restrictions in the government bond market or not being able to fund government debt.

The second critical intervention happened just over a decade later. It came not from Japan, but from across the Pacific. The result has created an alliance for change between core institutions of the American state, notably the Treasury Department, and the domestic Japanese interests favouring reform. This intervention culminated in what is most commonly called the 'Yen/Dollar Agreement' of May 1984, the landmark accord in the reform of Japanese financial markets. In Bergsten's words: 'The negotiations between the United States and Japan during 1983–84 over liberalisation of the Japanese capital markets . . . . were a unique event in the history of international economic policy. Pressure from one country on another to liberalise its markets is common in trade policy, but never before has one country so pressed another to integrate its financial markets with the rest of the world and to internationalise its currency.'[76]

The origins of American pressure lie in the challenge from the Japanese economy to the power and competitiveness of the United States. The signs of this challenge are numerous: the penetration of American domestic markets by Japanese manufacturing exports; the displacement of American by Japanese institutions in leading positions in world financial services industries; the emergence in the 1980s of Japan as an exporter of capital on a historically unprecedented scale; and the concurrent decline of the United States into a condition of indebtedness.[77] The American response was compounded of many elements: protectionist sentiments, manifested in periodic Congressional moves to exclude Japanese institutions from

American markets in manufacturing and in financial services; a determination to force the Japanese to realign the Yen, in the belief that the exchange rate had been deliberately manipulated to give Japanese firms an unfair advantage in international competitive struggles; and a determination to force the Japanese to open their financial markets to the largest American firms, in the conviction that the United States enjoys a comparative advantage over Japan in the financial services sector.[78]

The alliance between key state agencies and the big financial services firms was symbolised by the figure of Donald Regan, the former head of the great securities firm of Merrill Lynch, who became President Reagan's Treasury Secretary. Regan was, we shall see, a key figure in the negotiations leading up to the May 1984 agreement. But it should be emphasised that Regan symbolised an *alliance* between Washington and Wall Street, not the capture of one by the other. The firms had an interest in breaking down the barriers to foreign entry to lucrative Japanese domestic markets. The Treasury had an overwhelming interest in persuading the Japanese to ease these barriers in order to head off protectionist sentiment in the United States. The conduct of Reaganite economic policy depended on continuing access to Japanese financial markets. The heart of 'Reaganism' was the creation of an extraordinary volume of Federal debt. That debt in turn was fundable only through the willingness of Japanese firms to put the savings of Japanese investors into Treasury bonds: 'whereas the Japanese purchases of Treasury bonds amounted to only $197 milion in 1976, in April 1986 alone the figure was $138 billion.'[79]

Japan's emergence as an exporter of capital, and as a large-scale funder of American public debt, thus created a powerful interest in the reform of Japanese financial markets within the American state itself. An initial list of demands on the Japanese was prepared by the Treasury Department in October 1983. The centrality of the issue is shown by the fact that it formed an important part of the agenda at the summit between President Reagan and Prime Minister Nakasone in Japan in November of the same year. The result was an agreement of 10 November 1983 between Treasury Secretary Regan and Finance Minister Takeshita, in which Japan agreed to implement a range of measures designed to open up its domestic financial markets to foreign competition. The implementation of these was to be overseen by a joint Yen/Dollar Working Group co-chaired by a US Treasury official and a MOF Vice-Minister (senior civil servant).[80] Between then and March the group met six times without, in American eyes, making satisfactory progress. In March 1984 Treasury Secretary Regan revisited Tokyo and began to apply ferocious presssure for reform. His style can be gauged from his presentation on March 24 to a group of leading Japanese businessmen at a meeting sponsored by the Keidanren (the association for Japanese corporate leaders). Abandoning the circumlocutions of diplomatic politeness he reverted to the driving and brutal style that had made him a legend on Wall Street:

> Your markets are not open to our financial institutions. Your markets are not open to the capital for the rest of the world to enjoy as is the United States market, and the message that I'm giving to your Ministry of Finance, to others, is not a new message. It's a message that I've been delivering for three years now, and people have been saying to me: Patience, Patience. I'm about to run out of patience. I've had this now for three-and-a-half years. How much more patience do you want? My response is: action, action, action, that's what I want now. I'm through with patience.

He went on to emphasise the difficulties of resisting protectionist forces in the United States:

> How can we resist the forces, the opposition party, the members of Congress, your opposite numbers who are saying: build a wall up and fence in the United States. Don't let those imports come in from other nations, whether it's the EC or Japan or where. Keep our capital at home. Don't let people borrow in our market.[81]

The outcome of this plain speaking was the report of the Yen/Dollar Working Group presented in May 1984. That report did three things.[82] First, it committed the Japanese to a timed programme easing restrictions on US entry into trust banking and into the most lucrative bond markets. Second, it contained a commitment to examine liberalisation of interest rates and the removal of restrictions against entry to other markets, like those on the Tokyo Stock Exchange. As we saw earlier there has been substantial progress on these matters. The third and final feature was a provision for continuing discussions in the Yen/Dollar Committee on the implementation of the proposals. Thus the United States acquired a permanent forum in which it could legitimately intervene in domestic Japanes debates about regulatory change. (The group was renamed the 'Japan/US Working Group on Financial Relations' in May 1988.)[83]

Among those with economic expertise there is considerable doubt about the wisdom of the American strategy. There are arguments over whether the Yen has indeed been undervalued; over whether, if it has been undervalued, the integration of the Japanese into world markets and the internationalisation of the Yen is the appropriate solution to the problem; and over whether American financial services firms really do have a comparative advantage over their Japanese rivals.[84] Beyond these arguments, however, one point seems certain. The American state's intervention was in an exact sense 'critical': it marked a turning point in the history of the Japanese – and therefore the world – financial services revolution. This was not because American power was able to steamroller Japanese opposition, but because American intevention decisively altered the balance between the domestic coalitions formed in the Japanese arguments about reform. We know that as early as the 1970s the rigid Japanese financial structure began to break up. But we also know that the complexity of the interests lodged inside the key institutional actors – like the multi-bureau MOF and the multi-member industrial trade associations – made the construction of a stable reforming coalition virtually impossible, and caused the process of regulatory change to grind forward in a slow and tortuous way. The Financial Accord of 1984 changed that by adding a new set of (American) interests to reform debates – interests that were often voiced, as Treasury Secretary Regan's words of March 1984 show, with a most un-Japanese directness.

The years since 1984 have seen a prolonged and continuing 'financial services trade war'.[85] The main parties have been Japan and the United States, but the struggle for access to Japanese markets has also drawn into the conflicts state agencies from Britain, Germany and other nations with significant financial services sectors. The main weapon has been the reciprocity clause – the threat by host states to withold or withdraw trading permission from Japanese firms unless access to Japanese markets is given to their own champions. Thus the West Germans threatened to exclude Japanese institutions from Eurobond Deutschmark issues unless their own 'universal' banks were allowed into the Japanese securities markets.[86] The British Financial Services Act also contains a reciprocity clause which was used by senior government officials to bargain for the admission of British firms to membership of the Tokyo Stock Exchange. At the same time, it was made clear informally that the issue to Japanese firms of licences to enter the newly organised gilt-edged market in London depended on a satisfactory outcome of the British applications.[87]

The 1984 Financial Accord, and the continuing financial services trade war, emphasise yet again how incompletely 'deregulation' sums up the nature of the financial services revolution. Certainly many barriers are being dismantled, but this has little to do with rolling back the state in the face of the market. Regulatory change is being produced by hard bargaining in which state agencies are dominant participants. In Japan as elsewhere, the institutions of the state are key organising actors; and as in the United States and Britain the emergence of a winning reforming coalition has depended on interventions by state institutions. States have thus not retreated; their importance is increasing as regulatory change is shaped by the struggle for competitive advantage. The politicisation of financial regulation is as a result growing. In the United States and the United Kingdom this spilled over into the regulation of insider dealing; we will now observe similar effects in Japan.

5   INSIDER TRADING AND MESO-CORPORATISM

We saw in the cases of the United States and the United Kingdom that the regulation of insider trading followed similar trajectories, though not simultaneously. In the comparatively recent past, in both countries, dealing on the basis of privileged inside information was a widely-accepted custom; and in both systems insider dealing was steadily subjected to growing controls and more rigorous enforcement. By the 1980s it had become a major source of scandals in financial services. These scandals were a sign that one of the pillars of business autonomy – the unchallenged assumption that markets had the right to organise their own affairs – was under attack; and with this attack went politicisation and a growth in the extent to which meso-corporatism was codified, institutionalised and juridified.

The single most remarkable feature of the Japanese case is the extent to which this sequence has been reproduced, but in a compressed interval of time and with even more explosive political consequences. By the end of the 1980s Japanese insider trading regulation remained considerably less rigorous than in Britain, let alone by comparison with the United States; but the speed with which regulatory norms changed in Tokyo was so swift that it enmeshed leading elite groups in highly damaging scandals.

Japan lags behind the United States and the United Kingdom for a simple reason: Japanese standards have risen but from a level which, by Anglo-American standards, was remarkably low. Observers such as Strange have recently regretted the opening up of Japanese markets to Western-style 'casino capitalism'.[88] But Japanese markets have historically been, precisely, casinos – and, in British and American terms, casinos where trading took place in remarkably dishonest ways. This tradition has its origin in the first Japanese exchanges, which traded contracts that gambled on the future price of staple commodities like rice. The formal creation in the late 1870s of securities exchanges modelled on foreign practice made no essential difference. The exchanges were privately controlled bodies whose purpose was to organise arenas for particular sorts of gambling, not to provide funds for industrial investment: 'the class with capital came to shun the stock market, considering it as an arena for speculators.'[89]

The Americanisation of regulation attempted in the securities legislation of 1948 made little difference to this state of affairs. That law reproduced the anti-fraud and the disclosure provisions of the American New Deal legislation, both of which were to be successfully used by the SEC in its later campaigns against insider dealing. The Japanese behaved differently. We already know that they abolished the SEC-like enforcement agency wished on them by the Occupation forces, transferring its functions to the Ministry of Finance. The Ministry rarely used the anti-fraud provisions of the 1948 Law, and never used them to control insider dealing: in the three decades after 1948 there was not a single prosecution.[90]

There is a striking post-war contrast even with a centre like London, which was itself slow to accept the notion of effective enforcement. We saw in Chapter 3 that by 1973 the City elite had concluded that only legal intervention could control insider dealing. Yet near the end of the 1970s the Japanese Securities Exchange Council – a forum sponsored by the MOF for the most important industrial interests – still held the view that 'it is sufficient to make people recognise that insider trading is immoral because the new morality will then become the basis of practice'.[91]

It might nevertheless be conjectured that this state of affairs was compatible with effective regulation. Japan is a nation where lawyers are comparatively few in number, where there is strong cultural resistance to the use of courts as a way of settling disputes, and where public agencies prefer to intervene through the discretionary and nominally voluntary device of adminstrative guidance. It is thus possible that effective control over insider dealing happened in a way unimaginable in a more litigious culture like that of the United States. There exist, however, two important grounds for rejecting this line of reasoning: Japanese regulators are not equipped to control insider dealing; and there is overwhelming evidence that the practice has, until very recently, flourished in the Japanese markets. The Ministry of Finance has never had the personnel resources to track dealing patterns adequately, an essential prerequisite of effective detection. In the early 1970s, when developments in the United States first aroused Japanese interest in the issue, the MOF created a three-member 'watchdog', which delegated the task of surveillance to the individual exchanges.[92] Even in 1988, as insider scandal cases accumulated, the Ministry of Finance had only 140 investigative staff; the US Securities and Exchange Commission, by contrast, possessed 600. The detection capacity of the existing institutions had, in any case, already been fatally damaged in 1953 when the authorities amended the 1948 Law to remove the obligation upon corporate insiders to disclose their dealings publicly.[93]

The regulatory history in Japan, far from suggesting effective enforcement, indicates the contrary: a widespread indifference to activities long since criminalised in New York and London. Dore summarises the reality with remarkably temperate language: 'the stock exchange has never been a savoury place in Japan.'[94]

The history of Japanese financial markets has already given us some clue to the forces shaping what, by modern Anglo-American standards, are unsavoury practices. Before the post-war occupation securities exchanges were privately organised gambling institutions. The reforms of 1948, designed to 'Americanise' the Japanese system, were supposed to create bodies subject to public scrutiny and control in which prudent private citizens could confidently invest. For a short time at the beginning of the 1950s the majority of shares were indeed held by private individuals: in 1950 just over 60 per cent of share ownership was accounted for in this way. The situation has now altered greatly: by the mid-1980s the corresponding figure was only 25 per cent.[95] A similar transfer of ownership from private to institutional hands took place in London and New York, but whereas in those centres the rise of institutional shareholders reflected the creation of a new set of economic interests, the change in Japan reflected the partial reassertion of old forces: 'The balance of the stock market consists of interlocking cross-shareholdings owned by financial institutions (such as life insurance companies or trust banks) and corporations.'[96] This structure of ownership links groups of firms in the Keiretsu, the more loosely organised successors to the Zaibatsu. Ownership is held less for profit or trade than as an instrument of alliance or control. Shareholdings are 'the expression of some other business relationship, not so much a relation in itself'.[97] They are rarely traded because they are an expression of business alliances. Thus trading is concentrated in a minority of securities. This pattern of concentration is strengthened by the domination of the 'Big Four' securities houses: on one estimate the largest, Nomura, is reckoned to account for 60 per cent of trading on the Tokyo Stock Exchange alone.[98]

The characteristics of the Japanese stock markets may thus be summarised as follows: they have a history more to do with gambling than with productive investment; there are few rules against insider dealing or price manipulation; there are few significant administrative resources for enforcing the exiguous existing regulations; and the markets are dominated by a small number of large institutions.

The outcome is entirely unsurprising: such regulations as exist againt price manipulation are routinely ignored; and practices long criminalised in London and New York are routinely permitted. A culture of criminality and semi-criminality marks large areas of the market. Practices such as the churning of customer accounts and the extraction of greenmail are common.[99] (Churning is excessive trading by brokers for a customer, with the sole aim of generating commission income. Greenmail is the practice of buying a block of shares in a firm with the sole aim of inducing the firm to buy back the block at an excessive price, under various legal and semi-legal threats.) Some sectors of the market are linked to the more conventional criminal underworld and to politicians. 'AGM operators' are financial racketeers who acquire shareholdings in big corporations; they specialise in disrupting annual meetings, discovering scandals in the private behaviour of senior executives, and blackmailing the corporation with threats of revelations.[100] The 1981 Commercial Code outlawed the practice of buying-off racketeers, but it is still acknowledged to be common. It remains common because firms are anxious to avoid harassment, especially as most members of the corporate elite are over seventy years old and find difficulty in coping with long, embarrassing public meetings (the AGM of Sony lasted thirteen hours in 1984). In 1988, ninety per cent of publicly-traded companies arranged to hold their AGMs on the same day in order to make the racketeers' task of disruption more difficult.[101]

The widespread existence of trading practices that by London and American standards are scandalous touches the most prestigous institutions in the market, and links them to the political elite. Insider dealing is closely connected to business funding of political parties. The party that has ruled Japan continuously since 1955, the Liberal Democratic Party, is essentially a collection of factions held together by patronage and money. The cost of politics is large, and politicians have responded by developing a range of devices for extracting contributions/bribes from business. One of the most lucrative involves the right to acquire shares at prices which, on the basis of inside information, it is known will shortly rise and yield a profit. (This, we shall shortly see, was the central feature of the scandal that overcame the markets and the government in 1988–89.) Shares are also commonly 'ramped' at the point of issue to achieve this effect: 'It is not uncommon for the underwriter of a new share issue of a Japanese corporation to instruct its brokerage division to commence large-scale purchases of existing shares before the new issue goes to the market, thereby ramping up the price.'[102]

Although it has been appropriate to frame this account in the present tense, at the end of the 1980s there were signs of an unexpected and rapid change in regulatory attitudes. The outcome is in part a repetition of American and British experience: the development of scandal; the sacrifice of public scapegoats; and a growth in the degree to which regulation is juridified, codified and institutionalised.

The emergence of scandals was astonishingly swift. In 1987 alone, after a generation of moral and legal indifference, there were four widely-publicised cases. The most important concerned Tateho Chemical and Recruit Cosmos. In the former case it was revealed that, shortly before the public announcement of the firm's near bankruptcy, insiders in the firm, and its own bankers, had dumped large amounts of stock on the market. The subsequent investigation found that there had occurred no offence under existing regulations, itself an instructive comment on the state of Japanese arrangements. As a result of the case, in October 1987 the Ministry of Finance set up, under its advisory Securities and Exchange Council, a panel of legal and financial experts to examine the condition of Japanese insider trading regulation. The report of this panel provided the basis for proposed amendments to the securities law published by the Ministry in March 1988. Critics of this measure are, perhaps rightly, sceptical of its likely efficacy. It nevertheless represents, by Japanese standards, a marked change of regulatory course. It explicitly criminalises insider dealing: the maximum penalties (up to six months in prison or a fine of up to 500 000 yen) hardly amount to punitive sanctions, but are nevertheless a great break with the past. It imposes on insiders (like directors) a set of disclosure rules governing their own dealing. And it gives greater powers to self-regulators (the exchanges) and obliges firms to police their internal affairs: for example, stock exchanges are authorised to suspend trading in offending issues, while securities firms must establish arrangements to prevent the circulation of price-sensitive information between their trading and their other departments.[103] In the introduction of the criminal law, in the more elaborate codification of the rules and in the growth of more formal institutional arrangements, Japan is following a path already trodden by the Americans and the British.

There is understandable scepticism about the extent to which substantive changes in regulatory and trading practices are likely to follow the essentially symbolic alterations to law. Nevertheless, developments that coincided with the framing of the legislation suggest that a sea change in Japanese practices has indeed begun to happen. For the very first time the courts have actually intervened to hand down guilty verdicts against stock manipulators.[104] The biggest securities firms have also begun to change their arrangements in advance of the law: in July 1988 Nomura, the largest of all, established a 'Chinese Wall' to separate its securities sales division from other parts of the firm, in order to counter the possibility of inside information being used in trading decisions. It has been swiftly followed in this by other members of the 'Big Four'.[105]

These rapid changes in rules, institutions and underlying attitudes are closely connected to the catastophic consequences of the 'Recruit' share trading affair that dominated the markets in 1988–89. The Recruit scandal is pehaps Japan's greatest post-war political and financial scandal. Recruit Cosmos is a conglomerate with big interests in property development. It was brought to the over-the-counter-market in 1986. As is so often the case with new issues in Japan its price rose sharply immediately after flotation. As is also common practice in Japan, before the issue leading public figures were allowed to buy shares, and thus to reap huge profits after the public flotation. The inquiry into the affair has so far identified seventy-six leading individuals in public life who benefited in this way. They include the head of the country's leading financial publishing house and the Chairman of Japan's newly privatised telephone company. The most damaging cases have, however, involved leading politicians. Three members of the Japanese cabinet (including the Minister of Finance) initially resigned, as did the Parliamentary Chairman of the Democratic Socialist Party, on revelations that they participated in the allocation of cheap shares to insiders in advance of the public issue. As a climax, in 1989 Prime Minister Takeshita resigned over revelations that the aide controlling his purse had benefited from the issue. The connections with politicians have mostly come through aides who, acting as 'purse holders', used the profits from the issue to replenish their masters' political coffers.[106] The Recruit 'scandal', therefore, links two features embedded in Japanese life: insider dealing and the raising of contributions from business to fund the enormously expensive machinery that every faction leader in Japanese politics has to maintain. (The aftermath of Takeshita's resignation shows how the appetitie for scandal, once aroused, persists: his successor was soon forced to go because of sexual indiscretions.)

It is possible that the courts will decide that laws concerning bribery were broken, though in Japan the line between a bribe and a political contribution is unclear. But one of the remarkable features of the whole affair is that this highly damaging financial scandal is acknowledged to have involved no breach of the securities law. In the words of the President of the Tokyo Stock Exchange: 'The transfer of Recruit Cosmos shares to inluential people, including politicians, represented no legal issue. It is not insider trading. Nor can it be established as a bribery case. Yet the public thinks there is something unacceptable.'[107] We witness again something very like the American and British experiences: the sudden condemnation of activities previously widely practised; the concentration of attention on a particularly noteworthy scandal; and the dramatic raising of regulatory standards, in advance of the law and in such a way as publicly to stigmatise individuals who were acting in accordance with the old established ways. Likewise some of the institutions central to this process are the same in the three centres: in Japan, as in the United States and the United Kingdom, journalistic investigation and the use of scandal by opposition politicians played key roles. In other words, part of the explanation lies in some of the characterstic institutions of a pluralist democracy which undoubtedly exist, in however circumscribed a form, in Japan. Yet plainly some other factors must also have been at work to explain the discrediting of practices that for so long had been accepted features of Japanese economic and political life. The most important new feature was concisely described by the head of Nomura, in explaining why the firm decided to construct Chinese Walls in 1988: 'the Japanese securities market needed to enhance its image in the midst of internationalisation.'[108]

As we saw in Section 4, by the closing years of the 1980s Japanese institutions were being rapidly integrated into a wider international system, and were developing especially close relations with American institutions and American markets. The story of insider dealing regulation in the 1980s is not just an American, British or Japanese story: during the decade there occurred a tightening of controls in virtually every world financial centre of significance.[109]

One of the most important agents in this process was the American Securities and Exchange Commission. Indeed the Japanese scandals and the resulting revolution in regulatory expectations were preceded by two agreements covering insider trading between the Ministry of Finance and the US Securities and Exchange Commission. These agreements in turn were only part of a series concluded betwen the SEC and the regulatory authorities of other nations, notably Britain and Switzerland.[110] We saw in Chapter 2 how insider dealing scandals in the United States had by the 1980s turned the SEC into an institution whose organisational mission involved detecting and hunting down those engaged in insider dealing. The interpenetration of Japanese and American financial markets, coupled with the Commission's determination to expand its hunting activities beyond American borders, created the conditions for the diffusion of American regulatory concerns. In the Japanese case this diffusion influenced both the general nature of the scandal, and the particular institutional remedies, like the adoption of Chinese Walls inside individual firms. It is possible to remain highly sceptical about how deep and enduring the attack on insider trading in Japan will be during the 1990s. But there is no doubt that the scandals towards the end of the last decade led to a marked increase in the extent to which Japanese regulation was juridified, codified and institutionalised.

6 CONCLUSION: SCANDAL, AMERICANISATION AND MESO-CORPORATISM

The Japanese case reveals in an especially clear way one of the chief themes of this book: that the financial services revolution, far from involving retreat by the state in the face of the market, is a competitive revolution substantially shaped by stage agencies. But the role of these agencies could hardly be further from the 'strong and smart' Japanese state of common stereotypes. State agencies are central actors in the financial services revolution; but the state is too disunited to act as the strategic manager of the Japanese financial services sector. Insofar as there has been a state actor with a clear vision of what it desired, and the brutal capacity to press for the realisation of that vision, the actor has been American, not Japanese. The Yen/Dollar Agreement was the single most important event in the history of recent financial change in Japan; and the Yen/Dollar Agreement happened because of fierce pressure from the American Treasury and its allies among the largest American financial services firms. In a lesser key, the Securities and Exchange Commission's commitment to the pursuit of insider trading in the 1980s was a vital contribution to the revolution of regulatory expectations that led to the scandals and reforms at the close of the decade. The late 1940s witnessed a largely unsuccessful attempt by the occupying forces to 'Americanise' Japanese financial services. What the occupiers could not achieve Treasury Secretary Regan and his Wall Street allies accomplished in substantial measure. Change was happening before 1984, but it was exceptionally slow; was bedevilled by the absence of a cohesive reforming coalition of the kind created so successfully in the United States in the early 1970s, and in the United Kingdom in the early 1980s; and because of this, reform was only wrung out of the system by extremities of danger, as happened in the government bond market when the state was pitched into a fiscal crisis in the 1970s.

The causes of the blocked, immobile character of the system have been evident throughout these pages. Japan's great historical problem – how to fashion a system of capital markets that would allow her to catch up in the race for world economic supremacy – led to the creation of a particularly entrenched form of meso-corporatism. The financial services sector became an instrument for achieving national economic goals. The failure to 'Americanise' in the 1940s meant that this traditional pattern persisted even after the cataclysm of military defeat. The interests encompassed by the system were so complex and contradictory that, despite the great structural changes produced by Japan's own economic success and the wider world financial services revolution, no stable reforming coalition could be created domestically. The 'private sector' was, and remains, deeply divided: between industries like banking and securities, between firms of different sizes, between institutions operating in Japanese markets and those whose business strategies tie them to world, especially American, markets. The state is equally riven, down to the level of individual Ministries, as we saw in the MOF.

But these factors themselves reflect a deeper source of stress. The competitive struggle itself imposes in Japan, as it imposes elsewhere, contradictory impulses on institutions. It is almost impossible to find any institution of which it can be said: this body stands consistently for (or against) change. The Post Office, for example, is commonly pictured as an obstacle to change; yet it was the Post Office, as a player in the market, that was a major innovator in the struggle for customers in the 1970s.

The fact that every institution of complexity is burdened with these contradictions helps explain why crises and scandal so commonly go with regulatory change. In Gourevitch's words:

Crises pry open the political scene, throwing traditional relationships into flux. Groups, institutions, and individuals are torn loose from their moorings, their assumptions, their loyalties . . . . Circumstances become less certain, and solutions less obvious. Crises thus render politics more plastic.[111]

But crisis is not only a mechanism of regulatory change; it also lies at the heart of the relationship between financial markets and democratic states. It is to the wider implications of the present study for our understanding of democratic state behaviour in the regulatory sphere that we now turn.

5 States, Scandals and Financial Markets

> Capitalism creates a critical frame of mind which, after having destroyed the moral authority of so many other institutions, in the end turns against its own.

1 THE PROBLEM RESTATED

The chief purpose of this book has been to describe and to understand puzzling developments in the regulation of the most important financial markets of advanced capitalism. The most striking of these developments can be grouped under four linked headings: the growing similarity of practices and of institutions in financial centres that once had highly distinctive regulatory regimes; the central part played by state agencies in the process of change; the way all this has altered the bias to meso-corporatism in financial services; and the increasing 'Americanisation' of regulation. There is immense pressure to equalise regulatory standards, whether these standards concern the capital adequacy of banks or the rules governing insider trading. This pressure for rule uniformity has in turn helped create greater uniformity in the organisation of regulatory institutions. In some cases – like the adoption of American style 'Chinese Walls' in firms – the diffusion of structures is limited. In other cases – notably Britain's reconstruction of regulation in the Financial Services Act – the shift towards an American pattern is dramatic.

The resemblance to American practices emphasises a notable feature of recent regulatory change. It is tempting to represent what has been happening as a world-wide convergence. The image of convergence suggests, however, that all the financial centres in question are moving, at a similar pace, to a common point. That is not so. 'Diffusion' rather than 'convergence' best catches the nature of regulatory change: there is occurring an export of regulatory innovation from the United States to other countries. A moment's reflection suggests the not surprising notion that this diffusion – rather like that identified by Hills in telecommunications[1] – has to do with the might of America, both economically and politically. This entirely reasonable interpretation, however, itself encounters serious problems. For at least two decades American power has been in decline.

The extent of that decline is disputed between writers on international relations; but the fact of decline is not challenged. In financial markets the 1980s were notable for the rise of Japan to heights previously occupied by the United States. Yet it was exactly in these years that the United States successfully exported its regulatory practices. Why should the diffusion of American regulatory practices have happened at the very moment when American domination was under challenge? To put the question more narrowly: if there is to be growing similarity in the regulation of insider trading why is it not the standards of the Japanese, rather than the Americans, that are being adopted?

This diffusion of American practices is linked to the key place of state institutions in the process of regulatory change. It is difficult to estimate how far the total presence of the state has altered in the markets in recent years. Some regulatory initiatives – like the abolition of legal restrictions on interest rates – do indeed involve a retreat from state control. Yet the global attacks on insider trading, the reconstruction of regulation in Britain under the Financial Services Act, the landmark American legislation of the mid-1970s: all these point to greater, not lesser, state involvement. More striking still is the extent to which regulatory change, even when it involves dismantling legal controls, is closely shaped by the ambitions and strategies of competing public agencies.

The central role of the state is in turn linked to the fate of meso-corporatism as a mode of regulation in financial services. The altered nature of meso-corporatism is in some ways the most puzzling outcome of all. In an age when corporatist ideologies were under attack in the party political sphere, and when corporatism as a mode of macro-economic management was widely discredited, the bias to meso-corporatism in financial services actually became more pronounced. There occurred greater institutionalisation, codification and juridification: the growing embodiment of corporatism in a hierarchy of formal organisations; the increasing elaboration of rules governing the behaviour of actors at all levels of the system; and the growing tendency to translate codified rules into statute, backed by state power and governed by legal reasoning.

None of these developments are adequately captured by that imagery of 'deregulation' which has proved so influential in policy debates. 'Deregulation' is quite inadequate because it suggests the wholesale dismantling of rules and a retreat from the regulatory arena by state agencies. This inadequacy is now admitted even by some practitioners: it is reported that when Mr Baker was US Treasury Secretary he prohibited the use of the word 'deregulation' and insisted that the process be called 'regulatory reform' – a label commonly used to describe other areas of regulatory change.[2] The term is, of course, perfectly accurate, but its neutrality quite fails to convey how far the changes in financial services are marked by distinctive regulatory biases. A more serious alternative is offered by the image of 'reregulation'. This does indeed try to capture the drift of change, but it is bound up with a cyclical theory of the regulatory process which in financial services is at odds with the evidence. 'Reregulation' is often a critical account of what has been going on. It recognises the widespread shift towards more, and more formally organised, regulation, and it explains this shift as a stage in a regulatory cycle: in market economies, technical innovation and innovation in market practices so undermined traditional restrictive controls that their widespread abandonment was forced on the authorities; but the freeing of competitive forces created abuses and excesses, leading to scandal and business collapses; new regulations are thus demanded to check these abuses.[3]

The evidence of the preceding pages contradicts this regulatory cycle hypothesis in two striking ways. First, the famous cases of 'deregulation' – the landmark American reforms of the mid-1970s, the British changes after 1983 – show that the 'deregulatory' moment was also the moment when meso-corporatism was further institutionalised, codified and juridified. The abolition of minimum commission rates in New York happened alongside, not before, the legislative reforms in 1975; the freeing of the London market after 1983 likewise happened alongside the preparation and passage of the Financial Services Act. Second, the scandals driving regulators to intervene cannot – as we saw with insider trading – sensibly be explained by the growth of abuses resulting from the end of restrictions on competition. They have to do with revolutions in regulatory expectation that – often with great suddenness – engulfed the markets, stigmatising common, traditional practices and forcing the exercise of controls over once perfectly acceptable customs.

The emergence of similar patterns of regulation in once distinctive centres; the reconstruction of meso-corporatism in a way that gives state agencies a key role; the Americanisation of regulation: neither 'deregulation' nor 'reregulation' adequately sum up these, so we need some other ways to crack the puzzle. We begin with two solutions that offer some help, but that in the end turn out to be unsatisfactory. These solutions locate change in, respectively, the preferences and interests of powerful private actors, and in autonomous state institutions acting as strategic managers of regulatory systems.

2   TWO PARTIAL SOLUTIONS: PRIVATE INTERESTS AND STATE STRATEGIES

Private Interests and Regulatory Change

It requires no subtlety to see that regulatory struggles in the 1970s and 1980s arose from battles for competitive advantage between private firms. The breaking of the cartel on the New York Stock Exchange; the abolition of barriers to price competition and to market entry in London; easing of controls over interest rates in Japan; the continuing battles over the separation of the banking and securities industries: these events have their roots in the way structural change affected the interests of firms and drove them to seek new markets. The resulting regulatory changes have accelerated other well-known features of structural change, notably the emergence of a small number of multinational financial services giants struggling for markets on a global scale. To put the argument simply: similar firms – indeed often the same firms – now do business in London, Tokyo and New York; the growing similarity of regulation may thus be a response to the common presence of powerful private actors.

This account illuminates much of what is at stake in the regulatory struggles summed up by the phrase 'the financial services revolution'; but the actual outcome of revolution cannot be explained as a response to powerful private interests. The striking feature of the three cases examined in earlier chapters is that private interests could not independently organise effective reforming coalitions. The interests of firms were so divided that change either ground to a halt, or happened with agonising slowness. The resulting stalemates had to be broken by the intervention of state agencies: the Justice Department and then the Securities and Exchange Commission in the United States during the early 1970s; the Office of Fair Trading and then the Bank of England after the interests on the Stock Exchange argued themselves into immobility in the early 1980s; agencies of the American state after conflicts between domestic Japanese interests slowed change to a snail's-pace in 1983–84.

This immobility arises from well-documented features of business organisation in market economies. In conditions of competitive struggle the common interests uniting firms are limited and fleeting; the construction of coalitions for change is an uncertain and difficult business.[4] As Zysman says 'even the constituent groups of a coalition are themselves political creations. The social groups used as units of analysis to determine interests are not entities embedded in the social structure waiting to take form.'[5] The history of associational activity between groups of capitalists is a continuing testimony to the problem of organising businesses to recognise and pursue common interests.[6] In the financial services sector rivalries between firms of different size, between those in banking and securities, and between those of different national origins have all contributed to the unstable and shifting character of business alliances.

It might be presumed that the rise of the giant firm solves, or at least alleviates, the problem of organising for a common purpose. Whatever the Securities Industry Association in America, or the Japanese Securities Dealers' Association say or do, in practice a handful of large institutions dominate the American and Japanese markets. Yet in key respects the giant firm only internalises the stressful and contradictory character of business interests. The recent behaviour of big securities firms illustrates this. The largest American and Japanese securities firms domestically support the separation of banking and securities, but in their global operations have crossed the divide between the two, thus undermining the very stability of the barriers that they defend at home. This is partly opportunism, but partly a reflection of the fact that big, multinational financial services firms, precisely because they operate in different markets, and possess a complex internal organisational structure, contain within themselves the contradictory interests of business. Firms, like trade associations, are systems of representation. They reflect the ambitions and strategies of their most influential members, and reflect also the tensions and conflicts of their different divisions, who operate in different markets, dealing in different products, under differing competitive conditions. Giant firms are complex organisations, and as such naturally stand for complex constellations of interests. Hammering out a common position inside a giant firm involves problems like those encountered in hammering out a common position across an industry: in other words, it is necessary to overcome the competing interests arising from different market locations, differing institutional structures and traditions, and conflicting personalities. As Hawley reported in his study of transnational banks (TNBs) in the Euromarkets:

The organisational complexity of TNB interests results from the banks' diversified, multinational (hence multimarket) transnational form. The resulting organisational flexibility implies the ability to shape or counter the unknown forces of markets and politics through diversification. But it also suggests the absence of a single grounded interest embodied in a unified organisational structure and purpose. What a single market institution could once define as interests located in one market or a few markets become increasingly internalised within a bureaucratic form . . . transnational enterprises are intentionally structured around bureaucratic units with competing (and often cross-cutting) claims, making 'interests' opaque. In ideological terms what are often taken to be the objective interests of business enterprises are in fact bureaucratic interpretations drawn from a broad matrix of often conflicting possibilities.[7]

There would have been no world financial services revolution had the outcome depended solely on competitive struggles and the capacity of firms to organise coalitions for change. In each of the three cases examined here intervention by state agencies was crucial. In some instances – like the American reforms of 1975 – the authoritative character of state power embodied in law was used to impose change on markets. In others – like the Bank of England's desertion of the Stock Exchange in 1982 – the coalitions for and against change were so finely weighted that a change of allegiance by one significant actor was sufficient to tilt the balance of advantage in favour of reform. State agencies are critical to the creation of coalitions for change in markets. The exploration of what in turn shapes state intervention has been the central concern of state theory in recent years. To this we now turn.

State Agencies and Regulatory Change

The recent revival of state theory has left us with two particularly compelling accounts of the role of state agencies in shaping policy outcomes. I call these, following established usage, neo-elitist and structuralist.

Neo-elitist theory insists that a clear distinction can be made between state and society, and thus between state and societal interests. To use Nordlinger's words: 'the state is autonomous to the extent that it translates its preferences into authoritative actions, the degree to which public policy conforms to the parallelogram of the public officials' resource-weighted preferences.'[8] States are institutions that can extract resources from societal interests, can use these resources in turn to control and shape these interests and can develop independent objectives of their own.

These accounts are neo-elitist because they stress the autonomous capacity of bureaucratic and political elites to pursue independent objectives based on conceptions of interest derived from their institutional location and from their independently formed ideologies. Krasner's formulation has proved particularly influential: 'it is useful to conceive of a state as a set of roles and institutions having peculiar drives, compulsions, and aims of their own that are separate and distinct from the interests of any particular societal group.'[9] State institutions can thus develop and defend a conception of interests and they can reshape the way private institutions perceive their own interests.

There are here remarkable echoes of the politics of the financial services revolution. Part of the story is the long-term growth in the capacity and autonomy of key public institutions concerned with regulation. When the struggles for regulatory change reached their climax in the United States in the 1970s, a generation of post New Deal regulation had endowed agencies like the Securities and Exchange Commission and the Federal Reserve with analytic capacities, institutional philosophies and able professional staff whose careers turned on the production of solutions to regulatory problems. The British case is equally striking. By the 1980s the Bank of England was dominated by its executive staff. It possessed, as a result of over two decades of internal reform, powerful professional resources. It used these resources to develop and defend a view about the proper course of regulatory reform. It even directly reshaped the nature of private interests by its behind-the-scenes interventions in the mergers and take-overs that succeeded the Goodison/Parkison agreement of 1983.[10] In brief: neo-elitist 'state theory' powerfully accounts for the key role played by state agencies in the financial services revolution. Unfortunately, it is very poor at accounting for either the substance of regulatory outcomes produced by these interventions, or the sequencing of state intervention. National state structures are unique: elite political culture, historical experience and formal organisation are all different in the United States, the United Kingdom and Japan. These differences plainly extend to the patterns of state organisation in financial services. To put it at its mildest: the Bank of England is a very different institution from the US Securities and Exchange Commission; and both are very different again from the Japanese Ministry of Finance. If state structures are decisive, the variability of state structures should therefore result in divergent regulatory responses. Yet we know that the most striking regulatory feature of the financial services revolution is the common experience of an increasingly codified, institutionalised and juridified meso-corporatism.

The difficulty of making sense of the substance of change is compounded by what we know about the sequencing of the financial services revolution. Neo-elitist state theories have not only emphasised the potential capacity of states to shape outcomes independently of private interests; they have also stressed the variability of states in this respect. Krasner's work was seminal. He argued that: 'Despite variations among issue areas within countries, there are modal differences in the power of the state among the advanced market-economy countries. France and Japan probably have the strongest states.' By contrast, 'America has a strong society but a weak state.'[11] The revolution in financial regulation has indeed been a state-organised revolution – but one inaugurated in a 'weak' state, the American, followed next by the British, and pursued only in a limited way by the 'strongest', Japan. The Japanese have nothing to match the ruthlessness with which the backward British stockbroking community was sacrificed after 1983. Indeed Japanese reform has depended, as we saw in Chapter 4, on pressure from central agencies of the American state demanding, in Treasury Secretary Regan's words, 'action, action, action'. In short: the 'weak' state led the way in the financial services revolution, and bullied the 'strong' state into reform.

Of course the limits of general characterisations of state capacities are well known – indeed are implied by Krasner's original emphasis on *modal* differences between states. But subsequent research has suggested, so great is the dispersion around any national mean, that analysis has to be disaggregated. Wright has summed up the present balance of evidence:

> Government is neither monolithic nor homogeneous, although it is fre-
> quently discussed and treated as if it were. Ministries, departments, com-
> missions and councils – governmental and quasi-governmental – differ
> not only in type of function – deliberative, regulatory, adjudicatory,
> entrepreneurial – but have different, multiple objectives and pursue dif-
> ferent strategies which often collide and conflict with each other. They
> possess different kinds of resources and deploy them differently accord-
> ing to the perceived objectives and strategy of dominant coalitions
> within them. More narrowly still, individual governmental organisa-
> tions are neither monolithic nor homogeneous. Divisions, branches
> and sections within such organisations may equally be differentiated
> by functions and resources, and by their ability and willingness to use
> them in particular ways to pursue particular strategies.[12]

This picture of fragmentation is, we know from previous chapters, a particularly compelling account of the state's place in the American and Japanese regulatory struggles. Yet it also returns us to the original problem: if state structures are fragmented, and business interests are so racked with contradictions, how did the reforming coalitions in financial services ever take shape, and why has change taken a persistently similar form in very different national settings and institutional structures?

One partial answer lies in contingency. It is precisely when interests in the markets are in conditions of stalemate that an intervention by a fragment of the state can decisively force a change. This is the significance of the intervention of the Justice Department in the American debates, of the Bank of England's shift of position in 1982, of the US Treasury's intervention in the Japanese struggle in 1983–84. Ikenberry makes the point writing in general terms about state agencies' contribution to adjustment processes:

> Even if a state's adjustment policy were directed primarily at the margin of larger international processes, it would be a mistake to diminish its significance . . . marginal actions stretched over extended periods can result in profound political and economic change.[13]

Fragments of a state can thus exercise an influence which, even when marginal, is nevertheless decisive because the intervention pushes deadlocked, immobile interests into motion. One of the added attractions of this account is that it brings us close to the contingent character of regulatory struggles – to the way they can hinge on the twists and turns of agency tactics and of the intervention at critical moments of particular personalities. Thus we saw in the British case that the Stock Exchange's problems owed much to the fact that in Gordon Borrie it faced a formidable and skilled inquisitor at the head of the Office of Fair Trading; and the resolution of these problems in 1982–83 likewise had much to do with the diplomatic skills and career ambitions of David Walker in the Bank of England. The frankness with which parts of the American state intervened in the Japanese struggles in 1983–84 also owed much to the 'action, action, action', mentality of Donald Regan as Treasury Secretary.[14]

A 'weak' state fragmented into quarrelling parts can thus still decisively shape regulatory struggles, because particular bits of the state can intervene to break the deadlock caused by the fragmented and contradictory interests in the firms that operate in financial markets. But if this makes sense of the twists and turns of regulatory struggles, it still leaves us with a great gap in the explanation. The financial services revolution has a world-wide pattern – the growing codification, institutionalisation and juridification of meso-corporatism. Why should contingent interventions by fragmented agencies, operating in different national settings, influenced by different personalities, nevertheless drive regulatory systems in the same direction? The question prompts the suspicion that, underneath the surface of everyday regulatory struggles, powerful structural forces are moulding the apparently contingent interventions of state agencies to a consistent shape.

This is, in essence, what a 'state structuralist' account would lead us to expect. Regulatory outcomes are not, on this view, the result of private domination of the regulatory process, nor the product of intervention by an autonomous state guided by a strategic vision, nor contingent on interventions by competing state fragments. States are indeed internally divided, but the fissures are connected to deep structural cleavages in markets. Regulatory change is the outcome of struggles between alliances that link state agencies and blocks of firms. In these circumstances public agencies are crucial in organising competing blocks, while the state structure itself provides both an arena of struggle and mechanisms for the resolution of struggle.

The most persuasive recent account is offered by Robert Cox. The actions of state institutions can indeed be independent of private interests, but 'state actions are constrained by the knowledge on the part of the state's agents of what the class structure makes possible and what it precludes'.[15] State agencies are not the instruments of private interests, but they are commonly the allies of particular economic blocks. As markets become global, so the network of alliances crosses state boundaries: 'the historic blocs underpinning particular states become connected through the mutual interests and ideological perspectives of social classes in different countries, and global classes began to form.'[16] Now there exists a 'trans-national managerial class'. This class is 'not limited to persons actually employed among the managerial cadres of multinational corporations and their families. It encompasses public officials in the national and international agencies involved with economic management and a whole range of experts and specialists who in some way are connected with the maintenance of the world economy.'[17] Thus policy is more than a response to the demands of private actors. States 'determine the whole complex structure of production from which the state then extracts sufficient resources to continue to exercise its power. Of course, states do not do this in an isolated way. Each state is constrained by its position and its relative power in the world order.' A major constraint 'lies in the way the military and financial constraints of the world system limit the state's options and the extent to which its historic bloc is penetrated by class forces that transcend or are outside its own borders'.[18]

This account offers us a picture of regulatory struggles that makes sense of much that is otherwise incomprehensible in the financial services revolution. Regulatory outcomes are deeply shaped by the intervention of state agencies. Yet states are not actors guided by a strategic vision. They are constellations of agencies joined in alliances with constellations of private interests. The shape of these alliances is determined by the wider structural features of markets. In the case of financial services this has dictated the formation of cross-national alliances linking the largest firms most attuned to world markets with the fragments of states that, by virtue of their organisational culture or their place in the regulatory division of labour, are international in outlook. Japanese reform during and after the Yen/Dollar Agreement was the result of an alliance between parts of the American state anxious both to open up Japanese markets and to divert American domestic protectionist pressures; parts of the Japanese state anxious to reform domestic structures and to maintain access to American markets; giant American firms wishing to enter Japanese markets; and sections of the Japanese financial services sector anxious to maintain and expand its bridgehead in the United States.

One of the strengths of this account is that, by stressing the cross-national character of the coalitions for change in financial services, it helps to explain why national regulatory structures are showing growing similarities. More precisely, it helps explain why so much of the financial services revolution involves the diffusion of American regulatory institutions and practices, at the very moment when American supremacy seems to be under challenge. The character and limit of this challenge is well described in Strange's *States and Markets*. Strange argues that a distinction should be made between *relational power* and *structural power*. The first consists in 'the power of A to get B to do something they would not otherwise do'. Structural power, by contrast, 'is the power to shape and determine the structures of the global political economy within which other states, their political institutions, their economic enterprises and (not least) their scientists and other professional people have to operate'.[19] American power has indeed declined in a relational sense; but American structural power has, if anything, grown. There are four key sources of this structural power: 'control over security; control over production; control over credit; and control over knowledge, beliefs and ideas'.[20] It is the central position of the American state and American corporations in the four interrelated structures of the international system – security, finance, production and knowledge – that is the source of American structural power: 'the gap between US power and that of any rival state when it comes to exercising influence over the basic structures is still so substantial that no initiative has yet been taken in international organisations that the United States has persistently resisted, while most of the (comparatively rare) initiatives that have been taken by the United States are in fact executed by international organisations.'[21]

Strange's arguments greatly clarify two otherwise puzzling features of the financial services revolution: the growing similarity of regulatory structures; and the pattern by which regulatory change is being diffused. The similarity of regulatory structures amounts to a partial 'Americanisation'. This is to be expected when the cross-national alliances for change are created in an international system characterised by deep and pervasive

American power. The 'Americanisation' of regulation is correspondingly deep and pervasive. It is reflected in obvious, large-scale institutional adaptation, like the British reforms that – via the Securities and Investments Board and the self-regulatory organisations – try to transplant American arrangements into a British environment. It is reflected in the adaptation of regulatory structures at the micro-level, like the construction in both British and Japanese firms of American-style Chinese Walls, designed to regulate conflicts of interest. It is reflected in the world-wide politicisation of 'insider dealing', and in the use of insider dealing scandals to extend and strengthen regulatory controls over markets.

The mechanisms by which regulation is being Americanised emphasise Strange's central argument, that American power is embedded in systemic structures. The critical moment in the British reform struggle was, we saw, in 1982, when the Bank of England decisively moved to the side of the reformers. That move, in turn, was shaped by the perception that reform was needed to safeguard London's post-war position as an international financial centre – a position due to the City's success in attracting and retaining markets doing business in instruments largely denominated in dollars. In a more general sense the British reforms were also shaped by London's openness to American influences: to the presence of so many American institutions in London and to the ease with which regulatory ideas and personnel could cross the Atlantic. Of course the changes in Britain have involved adaptation, not mere copying. But the agenda of regulatory change in Britain was an agenda set by American events and American influences: by the competitive reforms in New York in the 1970s; and by the problem of how far London needed to respond by following American institutional patterns. The pervasiveness of the American model is shown by the way in which the very arguments about policy have been conducted: the differences over the role of the Securities and Investments Board, for instance, are differences over how far it should approximate an SEC-model, or to something weaker.[22]

In the Japanese case, the significance of structural power is even clearer, precisely because the international conflicts have been sharper: American pressure for (in Treasury Secretary Regan's words) 'action, action, action' is inseparable from the wider setting of American-Japanese relations – notably, of course, from the fact that in the United States lie the world's richest and largest markets. At a more immediate level, the world-wide crusade against insider dealing was spearheaded in the 1980s by the American Securities and Exchange Commission, whose organisational mission during the decade was heavily influenced both by an obsession with that practice, and by a determination to extend the regulatory arm of the Commission beyond American territorial borders.[23]

We are now close to the crux of our argument, so it is sensible briefly to summarise the case thus far. Neither 'deregulation' nor 'reregulation' adequately describes the world financial services revolution: the first is inadequate because it ignores the pro-active role of state agencies and is contradicted by widespread evidence of the growth of more codified, institutionalised and juridified meso-corporatism; the second is inadequate because it rests on a cyclical account of change that is at odds with the evidence. The view that the revolution has been shaped by private interests is likewise inadequate. The unstable nature of business alliances, and the contradictory interests embedded in individual industries, and even within individual firms, mean that firms cannot create effective coalitions for change. The proposition that states supplied the strategic vision missing in the markets rightly emphasised the central role of state agencies in the process of revolutionary change. It failed, however, to take account of the extent to which states have been internally divided in the struggles. It also failed to explain why the American state, so commonly seen as lacking in strategic vision, in these events proved a more decisive actor than 'strong and smart' Japan. These problems drove us to the realisation that the coalitions supporting the financial services revolution were cross-national in character, uniting fragments of the state, fragments of particular industries and even fragments of particular firms in a world-wide network. The alliance has been given coherence by American domination – both by American power within the financial services sector, and by the fact that the struggles have taken place within a larger structure of American international dominance.

By picturing the financial services revolution as an 'Americanisation' of regulation we begin to make sense of one last, unremarked, feature of the changes: the extent to which they increased democratic intervention in the markets, with damaging consequence for the most powerful private interests in those markets. It is worth insisting on this point because the imagery of 'deregulation' suggests the opposite – an escape from the controlling influences of democratic politics into a non-political world of automatically functioning markets. In truth the financial services revolution has deeply politicised the activity of financial regulation, and in the process is creating a regulatory world which is nightmarish for individual firms.

Three aspects of this nightmare should be noticed. First, and perhaps least important, it is an expensive nightmare. In London, for instance, one authoritative estimate in 1987 put the potential cost of the whole new regulatory structure at £100 million.[24] A second aspect of the nightmare is revealed by one of the recurrent themes of these pages – the codification, institutionalisation and juridification of meso-corporatism. The original bias to corporatism could, in summary, be said to have had the functions of keeping regulation simple and keeping it under the control of the people who actually traded in the markets. That is being lost to such an extent that even individual firms have, in their compliance departments and in their systems of Chinese Walls, been reshaped by the drive for more codification and institutionalisation. It is sometimes remarked that one function of economic regulation under capitalism is to create a framework of stability within which exchanges and competitive struggles can take place in markets. That framework of stability is decreasingly in evidence. The story of the financial services revolution is the story of the rapid creation of new institutions struggling for regulatory jurisdiction, the development of increasingly complex and unclear rules and the creation of growing numbers of regulators inside and outside firms, all quarrelling over the meaning of an expanding, contradictory and unclear body of jurisprudence.

This connects to the third aspect of the regulatory nightmare: markets have become prone to scandal and crisis with damaging consequences not only for the financial markets themselves but for the wider stability of the market order. The age of the financial services revolution has also been an age of scandal. Unstable regulatory environments with swiftly changing and uncertain rules have often left those actually involved in competitive struggles on the wrong side of newly-drawn regulatory divides. The paradigmatic case is the one examined in these pages, the world-wide campaign against insider dealing. A practice once perfectly common and respectable in financial markets had, by the 1980s, become a major source of political and financial scandal, the subject of a growing body of law, and perhaps the single most important reason for the increasing codification, institutionalisation and juridification of the meso-corporatist system. For any defender of the political power and autonomy of business the whole campaign is lunacy. The most powerful private actors, the giant firms, have no need of legal protection. They are perfectly capable of managing their interests in conditions where insider dealing is rife – as they had to do until very recently in London and Tokyo. The effect of the campaign has been to destroy the careers of members of financial and political elites; to publicise and to condemn practices deeply rooted in the history and culture of markets; to create a body of law which is unclear and probably unenforceable;[25] and to oblige giant firms to invest resources in elaborate internal surveillance procedures.

At the root of these highly damaging developments lie the competitive political pressures created by democratic politics, and what these pressures are doing to the old simplicities of meso-corporatist regulation. To these we now turn.

3 DEMOCRACY, SCANDAL AND THE FINANCIAL SERVICES REVOLUTION

The three nations at the core of the world financial services revolution are all pluralist democracies, but they are plainly neither equally pluralist nor equally democratic. The United States is not only the most important actor in the world financial system, and the predominant power in the wider international system; it is also, by a clear margin, the nation where open, competitive politics is most vigorously practised. Both the United Kingdom and Japan have, in varying and different degrees, the characteristics of pluralist democracies: but neither can match the depth, the range and the ferocity of open political struggles in the United States. America's distinctive regulatory culture is described thus by Vogel:

> The uniqueness of the American approach to regulation is the one finding on which every cross-national study of regulation is in agreement. The American system of regulation is distinctive in the degree of oversight exercised by the judiciary and the national legislature, in the formality of its rule-making and enforcement process, in its reliance on prosecution, in the amount of information made available to the public, and in the extent of the opportunities provided for participation by non-industry institutions.[26]

The sources of American distinctiveness are various. They lie in part in historically established cultural patterns and institutional arrangements: an egalitarian culture hostile to hierarchies and tormented by suspicions of secrecy; the social and economic diversity that fragmented elites and obstructed the creation of a unified ruling class; the institutional fragmentation of government that created numerous points of access and made the state structure itself a site of fierce struggles between competing jurisdictions.

This environment is, paradoxically, one of the reasons for the development of an early bias to meso-corporatism in financial services. The historical vigour of American democracy meant that financial elites lived in a dangerous world. Hostility to the power of bankers and financiers lay behind some of the most disturbing populist movements in the nineteenth century, like the Greenback Party and the crusade for bi-metallism.[27]

In the years immediately before the First World War – when financial power in London was still secreted in Lombard Street, and Japan was not even nominally a democracy – great financiers like Morgan were being denounced and investigated in Congress. Denunciations of Wall Street reached a crescendo after the Crash of 1929. The Crash and its consequences created an obvious economic crisis in financial services, but it also created a political crisis. Over 14 000 banks – half the total number – went out of business between 1929 and 1933.[28] The suspicion that this might indicate some defect in the prudence and honesty of bankers was strengthened by the revelations of stock market abuses in the public hearings before the Senate Banking Committee. Between 1929 and 1934 the political crisis in financial services consisted in the threat of control by the institutions of pluralist democracy. Meso-corporatism countered that threat. It created an ideology of practitioner-based regulation which put the markets in control; and it created a complex network of semi-public and independent Federal agencies to stand between the markets and democratic politics.

As we know from Chapter 2, this effort to use meso-corporatism as a protection against the wider, dangerous environment of a vigorously competitive political system broke down by the 1970s. Three forces were at work. First, as Heclo has described, the wider character of policy making in Washington changed as a result of the New Deal institutional reforms. The point of meso-corporatism was to keep control over policy in the hands of those who did business in the markets. By the 1970s, however, policy was being made in open and changing issue networks. In Heclo's words:

> Issue networks . . . . comprise a large number of participants with quite variable degrees of mutual commitment or of dependence on others in their environment; in fact it is almost impossible to say where a network leaves off and its environment begins . . . Rather than groups united in dominance over a program, no one, as far as we can tell, is in control of policies and issues. Any direct material interest is often secondary to intellectual or emotional commitment. Network members reinforce each other's sense of issues as their interests, rather than (as standard political and economic models would have it) interests defining positions on issues.[29]

This is essentially a more general account of the particular development in financial regulation that we noted in Chapter 2: the rise in the decades after the mid-1930s of a network of professional/bureaucratic occupations encompassing lawyers, accountants, economists, all of them able and willing to generate initiatives independently of the practitioners in the markets.

The second source of change, as we saw in Chapter 2, lay in the inability of meso-corporatism to suppress competitive struggles and the structural changes produced by those struggles. At the beginning of the 1970s financial regulation was already a pluralist battleground between competing organised interests.

Finally, the declining capacity of the meso-corporatist system to preserve the autonomous power of finance was damaged by the rise after the 1960s of a new wave of popular hostility to business. The shift has been well summarised by Vogel, whose account of its results in American environmental regulation is remarkably like the outcome in financial services:

> The contemporary changes in the pattern of government regulation in the United States cannot be understood apart from the substantial shift in public attitudes toward business that occurred during the second half of the 1960s – a shift rooted in the dynamics of the relationship among business, government, and the public. After more than two decades during which the American public was relatively supportive of the purposes and prerogatives of the large business corporation, public attitudes toward business became relatively hostile. Paralleling this change in public opinion was a substantial increase in the scope of government regulation over a wide variety of aspects of corporate social conduct: between the mid-1960s and the mid-1970s – the period when the major initiatives in environmental policy took place – more regulatory legislation was enacted and more new regulatory agencies were established to administer them than in the entire previous history of the American federal government.[30]

The effect of this shift in opinion was given added force by the particular circumstances of the financial services sector for, as we saw in Chapter 2, the terms of the meso-corporatist 'contract' developed in the early 1930s made the regulatory system highly vulnerable to critical analysis. The ideology of self-regulation suggested that practitioner control was better than more 'bureaucratic' arrangements. This pragmatic defence of business power was obviously open to the test of experience: any spectacular failure, like the 'back office crisis' described in Chapter 2, could do it grave damage.

In summary, the meso-corporatist system created in the United States in the 1930s was unable, a generation later, to protect the markets from competitive democratic politics. It is this exposure to democracy that explains the concern with scandal in general and with insider dealing in particular.

The workings of financial markets create numerous problems that are the legitimate concern of a democratic state. These problems, however, are of a high order of intellectual and administrative complexity. Regulation driven by democratic institutions in the United States demands something simpler: the dramatisation of problems in the language of crisis and scandal. These drives are intensified by particularly highly developed features of American democracy, summed up by Shils in a famous study as 'the torment of secrecy'.[31] There exists a passion for openness and a hunger to expose and to root out conspiracies. That passion and hunger were reinforced by the cultural shifts summarised by Vogel, and were given renewed force by Watergate and its consequences. Insider dealing feeds American passions perfectly: it involves secrecy, brings profits and is readily packageable in the language of scandal. It is also, set against the problems raised by the workings of financial markets, a trivial matter. But just as the most visible and 'scandalous' environmental problems are not always the most danger-ous, so the great financial scandals are not always about the most important regulatory problems. Politicians, Hall has remarked, 'sit at the intersection of a democratic electoral system and a capitalist mode of production'.[32] But other social actors also occupy this uncomfortable intersection. The managers of meso-corporatism in American financial services have done so for over fifty years, and by the end of the 1980s democracy's demand for scandals was a major influence over the way they behaved. Although insider dealing is a trivial problem, its consequences for the regulation of financial markets are by no means trivial. The effort to control insider trading, and the obsession with scandal that this effort represents, are a continuing source of changes in the character of meso-corporatism.

The success with which the obsession with scandal was diffused to other nations in the late 1980s was due to influences with which we are already familiar. In the United Kingdom and Japan there also existed a demand, generated by democratic politics, for scandal and crisis. The panic about insider trading that overtook Britain after 1985, and Japan in 1988, was closely bound up with competitive party politics: in Britain the authorities' response was influenced by fear of the political capital that the Labour Party might make out of the issue; in Japan the 'Recruit' scandal was a major weapon in faction fighting within the ruling Liberal Democratic party and in attempts by the LDP's opponents to end the Party's long electoral domination. But the British and Japanese campaigns would not have been sustainable from domestic forces alone. The vigour of British and Japanese democracy is no match for that existing in the United States, and the hostility to financial power is nothing like as sharp. What transformed relatively weak domestic pressures in the United Kingdom and Japan into something much more formidable was the growing global integration of markets. This integration, as we now know, is creating a system marked by the predominance of American structural power. There is a particular pertinence here in Strange's identification of one element in that power: the knowledge structure which 'determines what knowledge is discovered, how it is stored, and who communicates it by what means to whom and on what terms'.[33] The knowledge structure in financial regulation – indeed in economic regulation as a whole – is American dominated. In the study of financial regulation nothing matches the quality, the professionalism or the prestige of the work done by American scholars in American institutes and universities. Among public agencies, bodies like the Federal Reserve and the Securities and Exchange Commission are world leaders in their fields. Indeed, we have seen that the SEC has been a driving force in the creation of an international network of agreements to curb insider dealing. In the private sector also, regulatory knowledge and capacity are lodged overwhelmingly in American institutions – in the big corporate law and accounting firms, and in the regulatory divisions of the largest banks and securities houses. Through this knowledge structure American regulatory ideologies are being exported. Since those ideologies are in important ways damaging to business power, the world financial services revolution is, to put it mildly, a mixed blessing for the giant firms in the financial services sector.

We began with parochial concerns, so it is sensible to end in the same way. Our starting point was an astonishing sight: the British state, despised for so long as hopelessly bereft of strategic vision or organising strength, had intervened to compel the reorganisation of financial services, with the aim of preserving the UK position at the leading edge of world markets. Closer inspection, and comparison with events elsewhere, modified initial impressions. State agencies in Britain have indeed acted with unexpected ruthlessness to smash the power of lazy and inefficient groups, like the British stockbroking community. There was indeed something of a strategic vision in this, especially in the Bank of England after 1982. But the British financial services revolution turns out to have been a subordinate part – though an important part – of larger events: the penetration of American institutions deep into the financial services markets of the world; the challenge to that penetrative power coming from Japan in the 1980s; and the continuing capacity of American regulatory institutions and American regulatory ideologies to meet that challenge by reshaping meso-corporatism within and beyond American national frontiers.

Notes

1 Corporatism, Regulation and Financial Services

1. The most recent comprehensive description is Margaret Reid, *All-Change in the City: The Revolution in Britain's Financial Sector* (London: Macmillan, 1988).
2. Kenneth Dyson, *The State Tradition in Western Europe* (Oxford: Martin Robertson, 1980) pp. 248–9.
3. On the wider changes see, for instance, D. E. Ayling, *The Internationalisation of Stockmarkets* (Aldershot: Gower, 1986); on Paris see P. Cerny, 'The Little Big Bang in Paris: financial market deregulation in a dirigiste system', *European Journal of Political Research*, 17 (1989): 169–92.
4. Figures from *The Banker*, July 1989, p. 54.
5. See, for instance, *Bank of England Quarterly Bulletin*, 26 (1986): 373.
6. Figures from *Bank of England Quarterly Bulletin*, 29 (1989): 519.
7. Committee on Finance and Industry (Chairman: Lord Macmillan), *Report*, Cmnd. 3897 (1931), Part II, chapter IV; Yao-Su Hu, *National Attitudes And The Financing of Industry* (London: Political and Economic Planning, 1975); R. P. Dore, 'Financial Structures and The Long-Term View', *Policy Studies*, vol. 6, no. 1 (July 1985) 10–29; John Zysman, *Government, Markets and Growth: Financial Systems and the Politics of Industrial Change* (Oxford: Martin Robertson, 1983) pp. 55ff; Andrew Cox (ed.), *State, Finance and Industry* (Brighton: Wheatsheaf, 1986).
8. On the significance of trade in services, Susan Strange, *States and Markets* (London: Pinter, 1988) pp. 74–78, 104–8 and 171.
9. The figures are from *Bank of England Quarterly Bulletin*, 29 (1989): 517.
10. Robert Gilpin (with the assistance of Jean Gilpin), *The Political Economy of International Relations* (Princeton: Princeton University Press, 1987) p. 310.
11. Organisation for Economic Co-operation and Development, *International Trade in Services: Securities* (Paris: OECD, 1987) p.12.
12. Caryl Churchill, *Serious Money* (London: Methuen, 1987).
13. Susan Strange, *Casino Capitalism* (Oxford: Blackwell, 1986) p. 1.
14. Readers of Geoffrey Ingham, *Capitalism Divided: The City and Industry in British Social Development* (London: Macmillan, 1984) pp. 40–61 will recognise the debt this sketch owes to his work.
15. Two standard studies of the political implications of these arrangements

140

are Zysman, *Governments, Markets and Growth*; and Cox (ed.), *State, Finance and Industry*.

16. The organisation is described in: *Restructuring Financial Markets: Report of The Subcommittee on Telecommunications, Consumer Protection and Finance of the Committee on Energy and Commerce*, US House of Representatives, 99th Congress, 2nd Session, Print 99–DD, pp. 98–9.

17. This paragraph draws on Kees van der Pijl, *The Making of an Atlantic Ruling Class* (London: Verso, 1984) pp. 1–75; Charles P. Kindelberger, *A Financial History of Western Europe* (London: Allen and Unwin, 1984) part four; Ingham, *Capitalism Divided*, pp. 152–200; D. E. Ayling, *The Internationalisation of Stock Markets*, pp. 43–67. The figure for Britain refers to founder members of the Accepting Houses Committee and is in Stanley Chapman, *The Rise of Merchant Banking* (London: Allen and Unwin, 1984) p. 55.

18. The most up-to-date international summary is in: OECD *International Trade In Services: Securities*.

19. L. Gramley, 'Financial Innovation and Monetary Policy', *Federal Reserve Bulletin*, July 1982, pp. 393–400.

20. These events are documented and described in chapters 2 and 3.

21. The most accessible summary is in: 'Recent trends in financial regulation' in OECD, *Financial Market Trends*, October 1989, pp. 10–23.

22. House of Representatives, *Restructuring Financial Markets*, pp. 97–102 describes these.

23. 'The basic idea [of a futures contract] is to transfer the risk of price volatility from commercial interests, or hedgers, to speculators. Since the players only put down a small good faith deposit, called a margin, the commercial user is buying a form of low-cost insurance, while the speculator is taking a chance to make a potentially large profit': *Euromoney*, December 1983, p. 314. See also G. Gemmill, 'Financial Futures in London: Rational Markets or New Casino?' *National Westminster Bank Quarterly Review*, February 1981, pp. 2–13.

24. Stuart Valentine, *International Dictionary of the Securities Industry* (London: Macmillan, 1985) p. 67.

25. Ayling, *Internationalisation of Stockmarkets*, pp. 100–106 is a brief account.

26. These points are documented in chapters 2 and 4.

27. Strange, *States and Markets*, p. 89.

28. R. Smith, 'International Equity Transactions', *Journal of International Securities Markets*, 2 (Spring 1988): 19–31 (21).

29. OECD, *International Trade in Services: Securities*, p. 19.

30. Strange, *States and Markets*, pp. 74 and 171.

31. There is a large literature on 'financial centres' and their emergence. A useful, brief review of the literature is in H. Reed, 'The ascent of Tokyo as an international financial center', *Journal of International Business Studies*, vol. 9, no. 3 (1980): 19–35.

32.   The distinction between different levels (macro, meso and micro) is used to particular effect in A. Cawson, 'Varieties of corporatism: the importance of the meso-level of interest intermediation' in Cawson (ed.), *Organised Interests and the State: Studies in Meso-Corporatism* (London: Sage, 1985) pp. 1–21. The most important collection of essays in the original wave of theory is Philippe C. Schmitter and Gerhard Lehmbruch (eds), *Trends Toward Corporatist Intermediation* (London: Sage, 1979).

33.   Joel Krieger, *Reagan, Thatcher and the Politics of Decline* (New York: Oxford University Press, 1986).

34.   Peter J. Katzenstein, *Corporatism and Change: Austria, Switzerland and the Politics of Industry* (London: Cornell University Press, 1984); and his *Small States in World Markets: Industrial Policy in Europe* (London: Cornell University Press, 1985). The most important statements of American 'exceptionalism' are R. Salisbury, 'Why no corporatism in America?' in Schmitter and Lehmbruch, *Trends Towards Corporatist Intermediation*, pp. 213–30; and G. Wilson, 'Why is there no corporatism in the United States?' in Gerhard Lehmbruch and Philippe Schmitter, *Patterns of Corporatist Policy Making* (London: Sage, 1982) pp. 219–36.

35.   Claus Offe, 'The Attribution of Public Status to Interest Groups' in his *Disorganised Capitalism* (Cambridge: Polity Press, 1986, ed. John Keane) pp. 221–58.

36.   Cawson, 'Varieties of corporatism', p. 11. For extensive case studies of meso-corporatism in one key sector see: Wyn Grant (ed.) *Business Interests, Organisational Development and Private Interest Government: An international comparative study of the food processing industry* (Berlin: de Gruyter, 1987).

37.   See A. Cox, 'The Old and New Testaments of Corporatism: Is it a Political Form or a Method of Policy-Making?', *Political Studies*, vol. 36, no. 2 (June 1988): 294–308; and Cawson's reply, 'In Defence of the New Testament', ibid., pp. 309–15.

38.   Theodore Lowi, *The End of Liberalism: The Second Republic of the United States*, 2nd edn (New York: Norton, 1979) and Alan Wolfe, *The Limits of Legitimacy: Political Contradictions of Contemporary Capitalism* (New York: Free Press, 1977). Lowi rejects 'corporatism' because of its echoes of Fascism (p. 50); Wolfe wishes to confine its usage to what Cawson would call macro-corporatism.

39.   Charles E. Lindblom, *Politics and Markets: The World's Political Economic Systems* (New York: Basic Books, 1977) pp. 171–2.

40.   Cawson, 'Varieties of corporatism', p. 40.

41.   The image is from the (more historically particular) account of corporate bias given in Keith Middlemas, *Politics in Industrial Society: The experience of the British system since 1911* (London: Deutsch, 1979) p. 380.

42.   David Vogel, *National Styles of Regulation: Environmental Policy in*

Great Britain and The United States (London: Cornell University Press, 1986) p. 259 – a remark with reference to environmental regulation in Britain and the United States.

43. This argument is documented in chapter 4.
44. Peter A. Hall, 'Patterns of Economic Policy: An Organisational Approach' in Stephen Bornstein, David Held and Joel Krieger (eds), *The State in Capitalist Europe* (London: Allen and Unwin, 1984) pp. 21–53; and, more elaborately, his *Governing the Economy: The Politics of State Intervention in Britain and France* (Cambridge: Polity Press, 1986).
45. Cawson, 'Varieties of corporatism', p. 7.
46. My reasoning here is heavily influenced by Wolfe, *Limits of Legitimacy*.
47. Indeed, some of my analysis on insider trading is influenced by Levi's work on fraud: see M. Levi, 'Crisis? What crisis? Reactions to commercial fraud in the United Kingdom', *Contemporary Crisis*, 11 (1987): 207–21.
48. G. John Ikenberry, 'The State And Strategies of Mutual Adjustment', *World Politics*, vol. 30, no. 1 (October 1986): 53–77 (54).
49. W. Cooper, 'The Financial Services Trade War', *Institutional Investor*, November 1987, pp. 117–20.
50. Gilpin, *Political Economy of International Relations*, pp. 328 ff; and chapter 4.

2   The United States: Meso-corporatism and Industrial Change

1. The image of a licence or franchise is developed in Wolfe, *Limits of Legitimacy*, pp. 146–75.
2. Harold Seidman, *Politics, Position and Power: The Dynamics of Federal Organisation* (New York: Oxford University Press, 2nd edn 1979) Part II.
3. House of Representatives, *Restructuring Financial Markets*. p. 298. The quotation is a paraphrase of evidence from John Shad, then Chairman of the Securities and Exchange Commission.
4. *Ibid.*, Part III, chapter 1.
5. United States General Accounting Office, *Securities And Futures: How the Markets Developed and How They Are Regulated* (Washington: GAO, 1986) chaps 3 and 4.
6. John T. Wooley, *Monetary Politics: The Federal Reserve and the Politics of Monetary Policy* (Cambridge: Cambridge University Press, 1984) p. 7.
7. House of Representatives, *Restructuring Financial Markets*, pp. 98–9, n. 12.
8. *Ibid.*, p. 300.
9. There is a particularly good account of the expansive ambitions of

the FDIC in: W. M. Isaac, 'The Role of Deposit Insurance in the Emerging Financial Services Industry', *Yale Journal of Regulation*, 1 (1984): 195–215.

10. The origin of the regulatory system for futures is described in R. Anderson, 'The Regulation of Futures Contract Innovations in the United States', *Journal of Futures Markets*, vol. 4, no. 3 (Fall 1984): 297–332.

11. General Accounting Office, *Securities And Futures*, pp. 8–9 lists these.

12. The point is explored with respect to the evolution of banking regulation in B. Shull, 'The separation of banking and commerce: origin, development and implications for antitrust', *The Antitrust Bulletin*, vol. 5, no. 27 (Spring 1983): 255–79.

13. Figures from: *Restructuring Financial Markets*, p. 226; and (for investment banking) from the *Federal Reserve Bulletin*, February 1988, p. 93.

14. These were phased out in the 1980s after the passage in 1980 of the Depository Institutions Deregulation and Monetary Control Act. For background see H. C. Wallich and W. A. Warvel, 'Evolution in Banking Competition', *The Bankers Magazine*, November–December 1980, pp. 26–34.

15. The central significance of this to banking change is well illustrated in Gramley, 'Financial Innovation and Monetary Policy', pp. 393–400.

16. *Restructuring Financial Markets*, quoted on p. 299.

17. Stephen Breyer, *Regulation and Its Reform* (Cambridge: Harvard University Press, 1982) pp. 6–10.

18. For examples, the critical article by the then Chairman of the Federal Reserve: G. W. Miller, 'Equality in Banking', *The Bankers Magazine*, November–December 1978, 21–23; and Robert Segal, 'The Financial Ides of March', *The Bankers Magazine*, May–June 1980, p. 24–35.

19. For example Graham Allison, *Essence of Decision* (Boston: Little, Brown, 1971) pp. 144–84.

20. On disputes with the Federal Reserve, Anderson, 'The Regulation of Futures Contract Innovations', 297–332; on the dispute with the SEC see Commodity Futures Trading Commission, *Annual Report 1982* (Washington: US Government Printing Office, 1983) p. 23.

21. For this and other examples, David B. Robbins, 'Commodity Futures Regulation' in *Annual Survey of American Business Law* (New York: New York University Law School, 1983) pp. 867–912.

22. Vogel, *National Styles of Regulation*, esp. pp. 193–225.

23. M. Langley, 'The Influence Peddlers', *Wall Street Journal*, 16 July 1986.

24. For a glimpse of a 'sue and be damned' regulator see S Sporkin, 'SEC Enforcement And the Corporate Board Room', *North Carolina Law Review*, 61 (1983): 463–71. Mr Sporkin is a former head of Enforcement at the SEC.

25. For a fairly typical attitude see Commodity Futures Trading Commission, *Annual Report 1984* (Washington: US Government Printing Office, 1984) p. 3.
26. See, for example, L. G. Perry, 'The Regulation of the Accounting Profession and the Problem of Enforcement', *Journal of Comparative Business and Capital Market Law*, 7 (1985): 291–305.
27. Robert Sobel, *The Big Board: A History of the New York Stock Market* (London: Collier Macmillan, 1965) p. 235.
28. Milton Friedman and Anna Jacobson Schwartz, *A Monetary History of the United States* (Princeton: Princeton University Press, 1963) pp. 351ff.
29. W. Werner, 'Adventures in Social Control of Finance: The National Market System For Securities', *Columbia Law Review*, vol. 75, no. 7 (November 1975): 1233–98. The quotation, from p. 1240, is a contemporary reference from the 1870s.
30. For the origins of the Federal Reserve I rely on: Herman E. Krooss, 'The Historical Background of the American Banking System', in Herbert V. Prochnow (ed.), *The Federal Reserve System* (New York: Harper, 1960) pp. 1–19; and John T. Wooley, *Monetary Politics: The Federal Reserve and the Politics of Monetary Policy* (Cambridge: Cambridge University Press, 1984) pp. 30–47.
31. The ensuing report is: *Stock Exchange Practices: Report of the Committee on Banking and Currency*, Senate Report No. 1455, 73rd Congress, 2nd Session., 1934.
32. Of the large literature on the financial reforms of the early New Deal, Friedman and Schwartz, *Monetary History of the United States*, pp. 321ff remains an outstanding brief account. Two standard studies of the banking and the securities industries are: Helen M. Burns, *The American Banking Community and New Deal Banking Reforms* (Westport, Conn.: Greenwood Press, 1974); Joel Seligman, *The Transformation of Wall Street: A History of the Securities and Exchange Commission and Modern Corporate Finance* (Boston: Houghton Mifflin, 1982) chaps 1–6.
33. The quotation from Maloney (sponsor of the Act extending regulation to over-the-counter securities in 1938) is taken from *Report of Special Study of Securities Markets of the Securities and Exchange Commission*, House Document No. 95, Part 4, 88th Congress, 1st Sess., 1963 – hereafter, *Special Study*. The quotation from Douglas is in: James Allen (ed.) *Democracy and Finance: The addresses and public statements of William O. Douglas* (Port Washington: Kennikat Press, 1969) p. 82. This is a reprint of a volume originally published by Yale University Press in 1940.
34. Seligman, *Transformation of Wall Street*, pp. 72–100 is riveting on this.
35. Notably Vogel, *National Styles of Regulation*.
36. For the significance of the existence of a stratum of trained regulators

see, for instance, P. Weaver, 'Regulation, Social Policy and Class Conflict', *The Public Interest*, 50 (Winter 1978): 45–63.

37. Allen (ed.), *Democracy and Finance*, p. 244.
38. Jonathan David Aronson, *Money and Power: Banks and the world monetary system* (Beverly Hills: Sage, 1977) p. 47.
39. Aronson, ibid., pp. 71–9 is particularly good on this.
40. John S. Odell, *U.S. International Monetary Policy: Markets, Power and Ideas as Sources of Change* (Princeton: Princeton University Press, 1982) p. 361.
41. George J. Benston, *Corporate Financial Disclosure in the UK and the USA* (Farnborough: Saxon House, 1976); George Stigler, *The Citizen and the State* (Chicago: University of Chicago Press, 1975).
42. For this point with reference to staff in the Fed, see Wooley, *Monetary Politics*, pp. 64–5.
43. Seligman, *Transformation of Wall Street*, pp. 308ff is especially revealing on the organisational politics of the *Special Study*.
44. Lowi, *End of Liberalism*, lst (1969) edn, p. 124. This remark disappears from Lowi's revised 1979 edition.
45. Stephen Krasner, *Defending The National Interest: Raw Materials and U.S. Foreign Policy* (Princeton: Princeton University Press, 1978) pp. 56–8.
46. *Special Study*, p. 694.
47. The atmosphere, and the resulting burst of 'social regulation' are a central theme of Vogel, *National Styles of Regulation*. See also G. Wilson, 'Social Regulation and Explanations of Regulatory Failure', *Political Studies*, vol. 23, no. 2 (1984): 203–25.
48. Among the best summary accounts, for different stages, are: Lawrence G. Goldberg and Lawrence J. White (eds), *Deregulation of the Banking and Securities Industries* (Lexington: Lexington Books, 1979); Andrew S. Carron, 'The Political Economy of Financial Regulation' in Roger G. Noll (ed.), *The Political Economy of Deregulation* (Washington: AEI, 1983); Arnold Heertje (ed.), *Innovation, Technology and Finance* (Oxford: Blackwell, 1988); T. Simpson, 'Developments in the U.S. Financial System since the mid-1970s', *Federal Reserve Bulletin*, January 1988, 1–13.
49. For some 19th century examples see Sobel, *The Big Board*, pp. 52–53.
50. See for instance, F. Schroeder, 'Developments in Consumer Electronic Fund Transfers', *Federal Reserve Bulletin*, June 1983, 395–403.
51. The argument in these passages is heavily influenced by Gilpin, *Political Economy of International Relations* and by Strange, *States and Markets*.
52. A definitive account of American supremacy in telecommunications is Jill Hills, *Deregulating Telecoms: Competition and Control in the United States, Japan and Britain* (London: Pinter, 1986).
53. R. A. Eisenbeis, 'Regulation and Deregulation of Banking', *The*

Bankers Magazine, March–April 1984, 25–33 describes the devices.

54. For some examples see S. F. Bell, 'The Current Status of Multi-Office Banking', *The Bankers Magazine*, Summer 1976, pp. 43–9.

55. Chapter 5 explores the wider significance of these contradictory locations for the creation of coalitions supporting regulatory change.

56. See, for instance, General Accounting Office, *Securities and Futures*, p. 19.

57. For studies of the structural consequences of the 1975 reforms see S. Tinic and R. West, 'The securities industry under negotiated brokerage commissions: changes in the structure and performance of New York Stock Exchange member firms', *The Bell Journal of Economics*, vol. 11, no. 1 (Spring 1980): 29–41; G. A. Jarrell, 'Change At The Exchange: The Causes and Effects of Deregulation', *Journal of Law and Economics*, 27 (October 1984): 273–307.

58. A very clear account of the regulatory implications of the 1975 legislation is S. M. Miller, 'Self-regulation of the securities markets: a critical examination', *Washington and Lee Law Review*, vol. 42, no. 3 (1985): 853–87.

59. Securities and Exchange Commission, *47th Annual Report* (Washington: U.S. Government Printing Office, 1982) p. 314.

60. See Sobel, *The Big Board*, ch. 1.

61. *Special Study*, part 3–5, pp. 694–6.

62. Seligman, *Transformation of Wall Street*, pp. 281ff is authoritative on the American Stock Exchange scandal.

63. United States Senate, Sub-committee on Securities, Committee on Banking, Housing and Urban Affairs, *Securities Industry Study: Report*, 93rd Congress, 1st Sess., 1972, 85–033, p. 201. Hereafter, Senate, *Securities Industry Study*.

64. My sources here are Robert Sobel, *N.Y.S.E.: A History of the New York Stock Exchange 1936–75* (New York: Weybright and Tolley, 1975) pp. 303–305; and Seligman, *The Transformation of Wall Street*, pp. 384–90.

65. Seligman, ibid., discusses these judgements in some detail.

66. The most accessible version of the Justice Department's case is in: House of Representatives, Sub-Committee on Commerce and Finance of the Committee on Interstate and Foreign Commerce, *Study of the Securities Industry: Hearings* (92nd Congress, 1st Sess. 1971–2), Serial 92–37a, Part 6, pp. 3135–56. This series of volumes is hereafter cited as House of Representatives, *Study of the Securities Industry*.

67. Seligman, *Transformation of Wall Street*, pp. 411–12 describes the mobilisation of the economists.

68. *New York Stock Exchange: Fact Book 1983* (New York: NYSE, 1983) p. 52. See also Sobel, *N.Y.S.E.*, pp. 205ff.

69. Allen, ed., *Democracy and Finance*, p. 82.

70. This account is from the study by the SEC's regulatory division: *Study of Unsafe and Unsound Practices of Brokers And Dealers: Report*

and Recommendations issued as House of Representatives document 92–231, December 1971, pp. 206ff and Appendix A, pp. 219–22. The figurs for failures are from Seligman, *Transformation of Wall Street*, pp. 452–3.

71. Seligman, ibid., pp. 465–6.
72. House of Representatives, *Study of the Securities Industry*, Senate, *Securities Industry Study: Report*.
73. Seligman, *Transformation of Wall Street*, p. 405.
74. This account draws on Seligman, ibid., pp. 446–50.
75. F. K. Williams, 'Self-Regulation of the Municipal Securities Industry', *Securities Regulation Law Journal*, vol. 6, no. 4 (Winter 1979): 291–344.
76. Robbins, 'Commodity Futures Regulation'; Commodity Futures Trading Commission, *Annual Report 1983* (Washington: CFTC, n.d.) pp. 20 and 72–3; Anderson, 'Regulation of Futures Contract Innovations'.
77. D. Savage, 'Developments in Banking Structure, 1970–81', *Federal Reserve Bulletin*, February 1982, pp. 77–85.
78. The proposal for a super-regulator is over forty years old. It resurfaces at every point of crisis or scandal – including, for example, the aftermath of the Stock Market Crash in 1987. The history of the proposals and the various problems are evident in the report of the Bush Task Group, the last systematically to consider at length the whole structure. See: *Blueprint For Reform: The Report of the Task Group on Regulation of Financial Services* (Washington: U.S. Government Printing Office, 1984).
79. 'Paul Thayer Pleads Guilty', *Business Week*, 18 March 1985, p. 28; D. Baer, 'A Yuppie Fable', *The American Lawyer*, July–August 1986, pp. 83–91.
80. B. Morris, 'Arbitrageurs await the coming of the ice age', *The Times*, 11 March 1987.
81. The atmosphere inside the SEC is well caught by A. Bianco, 'It's war on Insider Trading', *Business Week*, 26 May 1986, pp. 24–5.
82. This was the single commonest reason I was given when I talked, in 1985–86, to a wide range of regulators and market practitioners in London, New York and Washington.
83. T. Hazen, 'Corporate Insider Trading: Reawakening The Common Law', *Washington and Lee Law Review*, 39 (1982): 845–60 (the quotation is on p. 847).
84. J. Cottrell, 'Insider Dealing in the United States – 1: The Law', *New Law Journal*, 31 January 1986, pp. 88–90.
85. Kennedy's business career is described in Richard Whalen, *The Founding Father: the story of Joseph P. Kennedy* (London: Hutchinson 1964) pp. 3–161.
86. G. Wang, 'Dirks v. Securities and Exchange Commission: An Outsider's Guide to Insider Trading Liability Under Rule 10B-5', *American Business Law Journal*, 22 (Winter 1985) 569–82; and Matthew Farley,

'A Current Look at the Law of Insider Trading', *The Business Lawyer*, August 1984, pp. 1771–82 for historical figures on prosecution rates.
87. A. Lewis, 'The unwinnable war on insider trading', *Fortune*, 13 July 1978, pp. 72–6.
88. Susan P. Shapiro, *Wayward Capitalists: Target of the Securities and Exchange Commission* (New Haven: Yale University Press, 1984) pp. 26–43.
89. This passage relies on Wang, 'Dirks v. Securities and Exchange Commission', pp. 569–82.
90. Farley, 'Law of Insider Trading', pp. 1771–82.
91. Donald R. Langevoort, 'The Insider Trading Sanctions Act of 1984 And Its Effect On Existing Law', *Securities Law Review* (New York: Boardman, 1985) pp. 187–212. There had previously been a disputed case law on futures and options.
92. Henry Manne, *Insider Trading and the Stock Market* (New York: Free Press, 1966) pp. 131–45; Stigler, *Citizen and the State*, p. 98; M. Dooley, 'Enforcement of Insider Trading Restrictions', *Virginia Law Review*, vol. 66, no. 1 (1980): 1–83.
93. The key documents are all in: Securities and Exchange Commission, *Report to Congress on the Accounting Profession and the Commission's Oversight Role* (Washington: SEC, 1978). This was a report for the Sub-Committee on Government Efficiency of the Senate Committee on Intergovernmental Affairs.

3 The United Kingdom: Meso-corporatism and Industrial Decline

1. Kindleberger, *A Financial History of Western Europe* chaps 12, 16, 18.
2. Bank of England, 'Regulation in the City and the Bank of England's Role', written evidence to the Committee To Review the Functioning of Financial Institutions, *Second Stage Evidence*, vol. 4, pp. 89–131.
3. For an authoritative description of the traditional style of banking regulation see G. Blunden, 'The supervision of the UK banking system', *Bank of England Quarterly Bulletin*, 15 (1975): 188–94.
4. The City's international character is particularly well described in Jerry Coakly and Lawrence Harris, *The City of Capital* (Blackwell: Oxford, 1983).
5. There is a brief explanatory guide to the legislation in C. Abrams, 'The New Investor Protection Regime', *Business Law Review*, February 1987, pp. 31–4/53.
6. An authoritative view of the theory and practice of the SIB is Sir K. Berrill, 'Regulation in a changing City – bureaucrats and practitioners', *Midland Bank Review*, Summer 1986, pp. 14–19.
7. C. Wolman, 'SIB bears brunt of City criticism', *Financial Times*, 29 March 1988; D. Brierley, 'City revolts against the regulators', *Sunday Times*, 21 February 1988.

8. Berrill, 'Regulation in a changing City', p. 18.
9. Financial Services Act, sections 114–6 and Schedules 7–9.
10. The most authoritative account of FIMBRA is provided by: E. Z. Lomnicka and J. L. Powell, *Encyclopedia of Financial Services Law*, Vol. II (London: Sweet and Maxwell, 1987, periodically revised), pp. 8–09 to 8–228.
11. H. White, 'Investor Protection and the Commodity Markets', *Business Law Review*, August–September 1986, pp. 219–20.
12. Lomnicka and Powell, *Encyclopedia of Financial Services Law*, Vol. II, pp. 8–229 to 8–777.
13. C. Makin, 'First Big Bang, now Big Brother', *Institutional Investor*, May 1988, pp. 58–67 is a brief account of the power implications of the new structure.
14. Schmitter, 'Still the Century of Corporatism?' in Schmitter and Lehmbruch (eds), *Trends Toward Corporatist Intermediation*, pp. 7–52. The quotation is on p. 13.
15. The most authoritative account of the different regulatory structures at the point when the 'City revolution' began is in Committee to Review the Functioning of Financial Institutions (the Wilson Committee), *Report*, Cmnd. 7937 (1980) chaps 21–4.
16. Committee to Review the Functioning of Financial Institutions, *Second Stage Evidence*, vol. 4, pp. 89ff (the Bank of England) is a good sketch of the range of regulatory regimes.
17. Quoted in Committee to Review the Functioning of Financial Institutions, *Second Stage Evidence*, vol. 4 (The Stock Exchange), p. 17.
18. Ingham, *Capitalism Divided*, ch. 7.
19. The social history for merchant banking is described in: Michael Lisle-Williams, 'Beyond the Market: the survival of family capitalism in the English merchant banks', *British Journal of Sociology*, vol. 35, no. 2 (1984): 241–71; and Lisle-Williams, 'Merchant banking dynasties in the English class structure: ownership, solidarity and kinship in the City of London, 1850–1960', ibid., vol. 35, no. 3 (1984): 333–62.
20. The historical background and the analytical issues can be found in : Sir John Clapham, *The Bank of England: A History*, vol. II (London: Cambridge University Press, 1944) pp. 95–102, 199–211, 226–34, 263ff; J. E. Wadsworth, 'Banking Ratios Past and Present' in C. R. Whittesley, and J. S. G. Wilson (eds), *Essays in Money and Banking* (Oxford: Clarendon Press, 1968) pp. 229–51; L. S. Presnell, 'Gold Reserves, Banking Reserves and the Baring Crisis of 1890', in Whittesley and Wilson, ibid., pp. 167–228; F. Hirsch, 'The Bagehot Problem', *The Manchester School*, vol. 45, no. 2 (1977): 241–57. The authoritative picture for the years immediately before the Great War is given by R. S. Sayers, *The Bank of England 1891–1944* (London: Cambridge University Press, 1976) vol. 1, pp. 2ff.
21. The account of Montague Norman rests on Sir Henry Clay, *Lord Norman* (London: Macmillan, 1957) pp. 278ff; and Andrew Boyle,

Montague Norman (London: Cassell, 1967) pp. 124ff. For the organisation of markets see, for example, Michael Artis, *Foundations of British Monetary Policy* (Oxford: Basil Blackwell, 1965) pp. 68–75 and 83–93; G. A. Fletcher, *The Discount Houses in London* (London: Macmillan, 1976) pp. 35–53.

22. Vogel, *National Styles of Regulation*, pp. 193ff.
23. The best study remains Michael Clark, *Fallen Idols: Elites and the Search for the Acceptable Face of Capitalism* (London: Junction Books, 1981).
24. The background is sketched in R. McDougall, 'Taking over in the new markets', *The Banker*, February 1986, pp. 42–5.
25. The quotation is from: Panel on Take Overs and Mergers, written evidence to the Committee to Review the Functioning of Financial Institutions, *Second Stage Evidence*, vol. 1 (London: HMSO, 1979) p. 4 – on which this account is based.
26. 'Judicial Review of the Panel on Takeovers and Mergers', *Business Law Review*, February 1987, pp. 29 and 57.
27. This rests on: *Proceedings* of the Tribunal appointed to inquire into allegations that information about the raising of Bank Rate was improperly disclosed (London: HMSO, 1958). (There is an analysis, using this report, of the social and economic connections between the Bank and City elites in T. Lupton and C. Wilson, 'The Social Background and Connections of Top Decision Makers', *Manchester School*, vol. 27, no. 1 (1959): 30–51). Committee on the Working of the Monetary System (Chairman: Lord Radcliffe) *Principal Memoranda of Evidence*, vol. 1 (London: HMSO, 1960) pp. 14ff.
28. I have tried to document this in two papers: 'Finance Capital and Pressure-Group Politics in Britain', *British Journal of Political Science*, 11 (1981): 381–404, and 'Monetary policy and the Machinery of Government', *Public Administration*, 59 (1981): 47–61.
29. Committee on the Working of the Monetary System, *Report*, Cmnd. 827 (1959) pp. 273 and 275.
30. The quotation is from Lord Cobbold in evidence to the Radcliffe Committee: *Principal Memoranda of Evidence* vol. 1, p. 52.
31. Select Committee on Nationalised Industries, *The Bank of England: Report, Minutes of Evidence and Appendices* (HC 258, 1969–70).
32. The origins and cause of the crisis are in Margaret Reid, *The Secondary Banking Crisis, 1973–75* (London: Macmillan, 1982).
33. My economic understanding of these events relies heavily on Maximilian Hall, *Financial Deregulation: A Comparative Study of Australia and the United Kingdom* (London: Macmillan, 1987).
34. D. H. A. Ingram, 'Change in the Stock Exchange and the regulation of the City', *Bank of England Quarterly Bulletin*, February 1987, pp. 54–65.
35. Ibid., p. 55.

36. Office of Fair Trading, *Annual Report of the Director General of Fair Trading, 1976* (London: HMSO, 1977) pp. 33–4.
37. Stock Exchange, *Annual Report and Accounts 1979* (London: Stock Exchange) p. 5.
38. House of Commons *Debates*, vol. 962, col. 305 (9 February 1979); Stock Exchange, *Annual Report 1979*; Office of Fair Trading, *Annual Report of the Director General of Fair Trading, 1979* (London: HMSO, 1980) p. 45.
39. Stock Exchange, *Annual Report and Accounts 1980* (London: Stock Exchange) p. 5; House of Commons *Debates*, vol. 972, col. 230 (23 October 1979).
40. Stock Exchange, *Annual Report and Accounts 1984* (London: Stock Exchange), p. 3.
41. House of Commons *Debates*, vol. 46, cols 1194–1203 (26 July 1983); Stock Exchange *Annual Report 1984*, pp. 3–4.
42. Office of Fair Trading, *Annual Report of the Director General of Fair Trading, 1983* (London: HMSO, 1984) p. 9; House of Commons *Debates*, vol. 49, col. 246 (22 November 1983).
43. *The Stock Exchange: A Discussion Paper* (London: Stock Exchange, April 1984) pp. 5–6.
44. *Stock Exchange Annual Report, 1984*, p.3.
45. L. C. B. Gower, *Review of Investor Protection: A Discussion Document* (London: HMSO, 1982). Goodison damned it as exhibiting 'theoretical coherence and tidiness': *Stock Exchange Annual Report and Accounts 1982* (London: Stock Exchange) pp. 3–4.
46. L. C. B. Gower, *Review of Investor Protection: Report: Part I* (London: HMSO, 1984, Cmnd. 9125). For the measured welcome to Gower see the response of the body then representing the main City interests: Council for the Securities Industry, *Report, 1984* (London: CSI, 1984) Appendix A, pp. 12–23.
47. Department of Trade and Industry, *Financial Services in the United Kingdom: a new framework for investor protection* (London: HMSO, Cmnd. 9432); *Financial Services Act 1986, Chapter 60* (London: HMSO, n.d.).
48. Gower, *Report, Part I*, pp. 17–25; Council for the Securities Industry, *Report, 1984*, Appendix A, pp. 13–14.
49. Berrill (a uniquely placed observer) remarks on these in 'Regulation in a changing City'.
50. The quotation and the details, are from the Governor's speech, reproduced as: 'The future of the securities markets', *Bank of England Quarterly Bulletin*, 24 (1984): 189–94.
51. Berrill, 'Regulation in a changing City'; and Reid, *All-Change*, which draws heavily on interviews with key participants, gives a glimpse of internal dissent (p. 246).
52. *Financial Services in the United Kingdom*, p. 13. The White Paper actually proposed two bodies, a Securities and Investments Board and

a Marketing of Investments Board. This strange arrangement was soon abandoned. For Hopkinson's views see, for example, David Hopkinson, 'The Coming Changes in Stock Markets', *The Treasurer*, December 1984, pp. 37–8.

53. Some of the most graphic accounts of change and its implications are in the Exchange's own documents; notably: *The Stock Exchange: A Discussion Paper*; Sir N. Goodison, 'Developments in the Securities Industry', *Stock Exchange Quarterly*, September 1984, pp. 7–8; and Goodison. 'The Stock Exchange at the Turning Point', *Stock Exchange Quarterly*, March 1985, pp. 7–11.

54. Emphasised by the Governor in 'Changing boundaries in financial services', *Bank of England Quarterly Bulletin*, 24 (1984): 40–5.

55. Their views are reported in 'The Choice of a New Dealing System for Equities', *Stock Exchange Quarterly*, September 1984, pp. 10–28 (p. 11).

56. Goodison, 'Stock Exchange at the Turning Point'.

57. The creation of majorities for constitutional reform still demanded all Goodison's persuasive powers: see, for example, 'City revolution: small brokers don't like it', *Investors Chronicle*, 29 March 1985, pp. 10–11; and 'Stock Exchange: Split over Reform', *The Banker*, July 1985, p. 5.

58. Reid, *All-Change in the City*, p. 26.

59. For the Exchange's own contemporary doubts about the extent to which the system could be defended, see 'The Choice of a New Dealing System for Equities', p. 11ff.

60. When I interviewed regulators and market participants in 1985–6, many emphasised Walker's role. This is confirmed in Reid, *All-Change in the City*, pp. 42–6 and 223.

61. Ibid., pp. 52–3.

62. L. Jones, 'The changing UK securities market: a Stock Exchange view', *The Company Lawyer*, 5 (1984) pp. 97–100.

63. The background is in Gower, *Review of Investor Protection: Discussion Document*, pp. 1–3.

64. *ibid.*, p. 137.

65. Jones, 'The changing UK securities market'.

66. See, for example, C. Wolman, 'SIB bears brunt of City criticism', *Financial Times*, 29 March 1988.

67. I have elaborated the argument in 'Thatcherism and Financial Regulation', *Political Quarterly*, vol. 59, no. 1 (1988): 21–7.

68. At the very moment when the Financial Services White Paper and the ensuing Bill were the subject of ferocious lobbying, I interviewed over fifty individuals in the City. I was struck by how little they appreciated the significance of the proposed changes even then.

69. The background is sketched in P. Farmer, 'Towards a Tougher Regime Against Insider Dealing', *Business Law Review*, December 1987, 283–6.

70. See Section 3 of this chapter.
71. The quotation is from: Panel on Take-Overs and Mergers, the evidence to the Committee to Review the Functioning of Financial Institutions, *Second Stage Evidence*, vol. 1, p. 21, which also outlines the contemporary regulatory history.
72. For an analysis of cases see B. A. K. Rider, 'Self-Regulation: The British Approach to Policing Conduct in the Securities Business, With Particular Reference to the Role of the City Panel on Take Overs and Mergers in the Regulation of Insider Trading', *Journal of Comparative Corporate Law and Securities Regulation*, 1 (1978): 319–48.
73. T. P. Lee, 'Law and Practice with Respect to Insider Trading and Trading on Market Information in the United Kingdom', *Journal of Comparative Corporate Law and Securities Regulation*, 4 (1982): 389–90; Council for the Securities Industry, *Statement on Insider Dealing* (London: CSI, 1981).
74. Lee, 'Law and Practice with Respect to Insider Trading'.
75. M. Cassell, 'Government may reopen insider dealing cases', *Financial Times*, 8 December 1986.
76. L. H. Leigh, *The Control of Commercial Fraud* (London: Heinemann, 1982) p. 11.
77. My account here draws on Levi, 'Crisis? What Crisis? Reactions to commercial fraud in the United Kingdom'.
78. Financial Services Act, 1986, Part vii.
79. The authoritative accounts are: 'The Bank of England and Johnson Matthey Bankers Limited', *Report and Accounts 1985* (London: Bank of England, 1985) pp. 31–42; and *Report of the Committee set up to Consider the System of Banking Supervision* (London: HMSO, 1985, Cmnd. 9550).
80. C. Wolman, 'The Collier Insider Trading Case', *Financial Times*, 15 November 1986.
81. As I write the accusations in the Guinness case are being vigorously contested in the courts. But from the point of view of regulatory change the significant matter is that the accused are charged with practices long common and accepted. Whatever the judicial outcome, therefore, the affair is a watershed. The Guinness affair turns on alleged share price manipulation and illegal and covert purchases during a take-over of the Distillers Company.
82. The recent history of insider trading control is reviewed in Mervyn King and Ailsa Roell, 'Insider Trading', *Economic Policy*, April 1988, pp. 165–93.
83. Levi, 'Crisis? What crisis?' p. 215.
84. Financial Services Act, part vii, para 175.
85. The details (based on the relevant DTI Press release) are reproduced in *Business Law Review*, November 1986, pp. 291–2.
86. Even by friends of the Conservatives: see *The Times* editorial 'Competition Not Corporatism', 29 July 1983.

87. *Fraud Trials Committee: Report* (London: HMSO, 1986) pp. 154–5.
88. For privately expressed doubts at the time see Reid, *All-Change in the City*, pp. 42–3.
89. The account of the Goodison/Parkinson agreement in this chapter draws on my previously published account: 'Politics and Law in Financial Regulation', in Cosmo Graham and Tony Prosser (eds), *Waiving the Rules: the Constitution under Thatcherism* (Milton Keynes: Open University Press, 1988) pp. 56–72.

4 Japan: Meso-corporatism and Industrial Power

1. Figures from *Far Eastern Economic Review*, 11 August 1988, p. 61.
2. The images of 'strong' and 'smart' are borrowed from Richard J. Samuels, *The Business of the Japanese State* (Ithaca: Cornell University Press, 1987), p. 1 – who analyses and rejects them.
3. James Abegglen, *Business Strategies for Japan* (Tokyo: Sophia University, n.d.) p. 71, quoted in Charles J. McMillan, *The Japanese Industrial System*, 2nd edn (Berlin/New York: de Gruyter, 1985) p. 44.
4. Chalmers Johnson, *MITI And The Japanese Economic Miracle: The Growth of Industrial Policy 1925–75* (Stanford: Stanford University Press, 1982) – the first part of the quotation is on p. 24, the second on p. 305. I should emphasise that Johnson's is a study, not of omnipotence, but often of the problems of realising developmental aims.
5. The 'administrative guidance' model, and its relation to other models of the Japanese policy process, is discussed in Yasusuke Murakami, 'The Japanese Model of Political Economy', in Kozo Yamamura and Yasukichi Yasuba (eds), *The Political Economy of Japan, volume 1, The Domestic Transformation* (Stanford: Stanford University Press, 1987) pp. 33–90.
6. J. Andrew Spindler, *The Politics of International Credit: Private Finance and Foreign Policy in Germany and Japan* (Washington: The Brookings Institution, 1984) pp. 93–134.
7. Zysman, *Governments, Markets and Growth*, p. 234; Yao-Su Hu, *National Attitudes and the Financing of Industry*, pp. 37–8.
8. Richard W. Wright and Gunter A. Pauli, *The Second Wave: Japan's Global Assault on Financial Services* (London: Waterloo, 1987). The first quotation is on p. 57, the second on p. 85.
9. Spindler, *The Politics of International Credit*, p. 110.
10. I was greatly helped in thinking out the alternatives to this prevailing model by reading Jill Hills, 'The Industrial Policy of Japan', *Journal of Public Policy*, 3 (1983): 63–80; and her study of Japan in *Deregulating Telecoms: Competition and Control in the United States, Japan and Britain* (London: Pinter, 1986): 100–19.

11.   Johnson, *MITI and the Japanese Economic Miracle*, pp. 26 and 310ff.
12.   George C. Eads and Kozo Yamamura, 'The Future of Industrial Policy', in Yamamura and Yasuba (eds), *Political Economy of Japan*, pp. 426–68 (esp. pp. 448–58).
13.   Michael K. Young, 'Judicial Review of Administrative Guidance: Governmentally Encouraged Consensual Dispute Resolution in Japan', *Columbia Law Review*, 84 (1984): 923–83. The quotation is on p. 941.
14.   Samuels, *Business of the Japanese State*. The first quotation is on p. 21; the second on p. 8; the third on p. 2.
15.   Michio Muramtsu and Ellis S. Krauss, 'The Conservative Policy Line and the Development of Paternal Pluralism' in Yamamura and Yasuba (eds), *The Political Economy of Japan* pp. 516–554. The quotation is on pp. 525–6.
16.   Bernard Eccleston, 'The State, Finance and Industry in Japan' in Cox (ed.), *State, Finance and Industry*, pp. 60–79. The quotation is on p. 68. See also Yoshio Suzuki, *The Japanese Financial System* (Oxford: Clarendon Press, 1987) pp. 35–50.
17.   There is a brief summary of the MOF's structure and functions in James Horne, *Japan's Financial Markets: Conflict and Consensus in Policymaking* (Sydney: Allen and Unwin, 1985) Appendix 3.
18.   The changing structure of bureaucratic power is a central theme of Eads and Yamamura 'The Structure of Industrial Policy'.
19.   Hills, 'The Industrial Policy of Japan' summarises the central role of the bureaucratic elite in economic policy making.
20.   Horne, *Japan's Financial Markets*, pp. 118–41 describes the jurisdictional and regulatory disputes for the late 1970s and early 1980s.
21.   This relies on T. F. M. Adams, *Japanese Securities Markets: a historical survey* (Tokyo: Seihei Okuyama, 1953) pp. 7–32, who also uses the 'franchise' image on p. 17.
22.   This is based on T. F. M. Adams and Iwao Hoshii, *A Financial History of The New Japan* (Tokyo: Kodansha International, 1972) pp. 37–41; Kenichi Shomura, 'Die Börsen in Japan', *Zeitschrift für das gesamte Kreditwesen*, 19 (1970): 924–8; Adams, *Japan's Securities Markets*, pp. 40ff. Some authorities refer to the 1948 Law as the Securities Exchanges Law, but Adams and Hoshii write of the Securities Transaction Law.
23.   Misao Tatsuta, 'Enforcement of Japanese Securities Legislation', *Journal of Comparative Corporate Law and Securities Regulation*, 1 (1978): 95–138. The quotation is from p. 99.
24.   Takahira Ogawa, 'The Japanese Securities Dealers' Association', in Hiroshi Oda and R. Geoffrey Grice, *Japanese Banking, Securities and Anti-Monopoly Law* (Butterworths: London, 1988) pp. 65–70.
25.   Adams and Hoshii, *Financial History of the New Japan*, p. 174.
26.   Michael Whitener, 'Japan tackles insider trading', *International Financial Law Review* 7 (1988): 15–18.

27. J. C. Wathen, 'Towards the year 2000 – Japan's emerging role in world finance', *Midland Bank Review*, Summer 1986, pp. 20–244. The quotation is on p. 20.

28. The passage on market management, relies on: 'New head of securities association vows to close ranks in fight with banks', *Japan Economic Journal*, 2/9 January, 1988, p. 2. For references to intervention in the 1987 crash, see *Financial Times*, 14 March 1988; *Japan Economic Journal*, 22 October 1988, p. 102.

29. Horne, *Japan's Financial Markets*, Appendix 4.

30. Hoshii and Adams, *Financial History of the New Japan*, p. 49.

31. Hills, 'Industrial Policy of Japan', p. 70.

32. Makoto Kawazoe, 'Financial Liberalisation Policy', *Japan Economic Journal*: Special Survey, Tokyo Financial Markets, 29 November 1986, pp. 5–7; Horne, *Japan's Financial Markets*, pp. 95–6; and Tatsuta, 'Enforcement of Japanese Securities Legislation', on the role of 'Auxiliary Boards' in regulation making.

33. Horne, *Japan's Financial Markets*, p. 210.

34. Ibid., p. 33.

35. Adams, *Japanese Securities Markets*, p. 7.

36. Adams, *ibid*, pp. 11ff.

37. Raymond W. Goldsmith, *The Financial Development of Japan, 1868–1977* (New Haven: Yale University Press, 1983) pp. 16–47.

38. Alexander Gerschenkron, *Economic Backwardness in Historical Perspective* (Cambridge: Belknap Press, 1962).

39. William M. Tsutsui, *Banking Policy In Japan: American efforts at reform during the Occupation* (London: Routledge, 1988) p. 4.

40. Ibid., pp. 8–9.

41. Katsuro Kanzaki and Misao Tatsuta, 'Major Statutory Amendments in Japan in 1981', *Journal of Comparative Business and Capital Market Law*, 5 (1983) pp. 249–66.

42. On the general significance of the inter-war period see Johnson, *MITI and the Japanese Economic Miracle*, pp. 307–9; and on finance, Horne, *Japan's Financial Markets*, pp. 26–8; and Tsutsui, *Banking Policy in Japan*, pp. 13–17.

43. Suzuki, *The Japanese Financial System*, pp. 305–13.

44. Eleanor M. Hadley, *Antitrust In Japan* (Princeton: Princeton University Press, 1970); and Tsutsui, *Banking Policy in Japan*, pp. 38–67.

45. Adams and Hoshii, *Financial History of the New Japan*, pp. 51–62.

46. Adams, *Japanese Securities Markets*, pp. 86–102.

47. Hadley, *Antitrust in Japan*, p. 59.

48. Tsutsui, *Banking Policy in Japan*, p. 124.

49. Adams and Hoshii, *Financial History of the New Japan*, pp. 492–3, on the special banks; Adams, *Japanese Securities Markets*, pp. 101–2, on the Commission.

50. Horne, *Japan's Financial Markets*, p. 28.

51. Suzuki, *Japanese Financial System*, p. 290.

52. Kanzaki and Tatsuta, 'Major Statutory Amendments in Japan in 1981', p. 261.
53. These details are from Adams and Hoshii, *Financial History of the New Japan*, pp. 165–72.
54. Suzuki, *Japanese Financial System*, p. 133.
55. Robert Alan Feldman, *Japanese Financial Markets: Deficits, Dilemmas and Deregulation* (Cambridge: The MIT Press, 1986) p. 8.
56. The quotation is from Aron Viner, *Inside Japan's Financial Markets*, (London: Economist Publications, 1987) p. 113. On growing strains see Koichi Hamada and Akiyoshi Horiuchi, 'The Political Economy of the Financial Market' in Yamamura and Yasuba, *Political Economy of Japan*, pp. 223–60.
57. This relies on OECD Economic Surveys, 1983–4, *Japan* (Paris: OECD, 1984) pp. 42–9.
58. This is drawn from Viner, *Inside Japan's Financial Markets*, pp. 189ff; OECD, *Japan*, pp. 45ff; Feldman, *Deficits, Dilemmas and Deregulation*, pp. 37–78. The definition of a Certificate of Deposit is adapted from Valentine, *International Dictionary of the Securities Industry*, p. 34.
59. Nigel Holloway, 'Finance: Markets suffer from tightly bound feet', *Far Eastern Economic Review*, 17 December 1987, p. 62.
60. Stefan Wagstyl, 'Out comes the buried treasure', *Financial Times*, 31 March 1988; and Nigel Holloway, 'Conflicting accounts: banks scramble as Japan ends the small savers tax break', *Far Eastern Economic Review*, 7 April 1988, pp. 99–100.
61. Ko Sakai, 'Government Bond Market: More liberalisation measures urged to raise foreign share', *Japan Economic Journal: Special Survey*, Summer 1988, p. 28.
62. 'Tokyo, Osaka vie for crown as stock index futures king', *Japan Economic Journal*, 18 June 1988, pp. 1–2; Hiroyuki Maeda, 'New Financial Commodities: New Packages to hedge against currency fluctuations', *Japan Economic Journal*: Special Survey, Summer 1987, p. 38.
63. 'Off to a flying start', *Far Eastern Economic Review*, 2 June 1988, p. 69.
64. Kyoko Hattori, 'Commercial Paper: Competition intensifies among banks, securities firms to lure issuers', *Japan Economic Journal: Special Survey*, Summer 1988, p. 24; on futures, *Japan Economic Journal*, 4 June 1988, p. 3 and 16 June 1988, p. 3. The definition of commercial paper is from Valentine, *International Dictionary of the Securities Industry*, p. 39.
65. Kevin Rafferty, 'The assault on Article 65', *Institutional Investor*, January 1987, pp. 133–5; Michael L. Whitener, 'The steady erosion of Japan's "Glass-Steagall"', *International Financial Law Review*, May 1988, pp. 11–14.
66. Shigeo Abe, 'Bond Offering Mechanism: Offering method subjected

to liberalisation to help open the market', *Japan Economic Journal: Special Survey*, Winter 1988, pp. 24–5. The quotation is on p. 24.

67. Nigel Holloway, 'Measure for Measure', *Far Eastern Economic Review*, 31 December 1987, p. 55.
68. Feldman, *Japanese Financial Markets*, p. 1.
69. Yuichi Ezawa, 'Deregulation of the Japanese financial market and internationalisation of the yen', in Oda and Grice, *Japanese Banking, Securities and Anti-Monopoly Law*, pp. 4–11.
70. Feldman, *Japanese Financial Markets*, p. 172.
71. A view which, for instance, deeply influences Wright and Pauli, *The Second Wave*.
72. This relies on Whitener, 'The steady erosion of Japan's "Glass-Steagall"', and Stefan Wagstyl, 'Time to play at home', *Financial Times*, 14 March 1988.
73. This is documented in: Nigel Holloway, 'Small Satisfaction', *Far Eastern Economic Review*, 28 January 1988, pp. 78–9; and Jan Rodger, 'Factions line up to test the barriers', *Financial Times*, 3 December 1987.
74. 'A challenge to Tokyo', *Far Eastern Economic Review*, 16 June 1988, pp. 108–9; and 'Tokyo, Osaka vie for crown as stock index futures king', *Japan Economic Journal*, 18 June 1988, pp. 1–2.
75. Wagstyl, 'Time to play at home',
76. C. Fred Bergsten, 'Preface' to Jeffrey A. Frankel, *The Yen/Dollar Agreement: Liberalising Japanese Capital Markets* (Cambridge: MIT Press, 1984) p. 1.
77. The most succinct collection of the evidence is in Gilpin, *The Political Economy of International Relations*, esp. pp. 311–40.
78. This relies on Frankel, *The Yen/Dollar Agreement*, passim; Gilpin, *Political Economy of International Relations*, pp. 331–7; Hamish McRae, *Japan's Role in the Emerging Global Securities Market* (New York: Group of Thirty, 1985).
79. Gilpin, *Political Economy of International Relations*, p. 331. Gilpin's views are confirmed by the more general review of the changing size and structure of public debt in Thomas D. Simpson, 'Developments in the U.S. Financial System since the mid-1970s', *Federal Reserve Bulletin*, January 1988, pp. 1–13.
80. This relies on the account given by Frankel, *The Yen/Dollar Agreement*, pp. 1–5. Frankel was, as a senior staff economist in the U.S. Council of Economic Advisors, involved in the American planning that led to the Agreement.
81. Excerpts of the text are in Frankel, *The Yen/Dollar Agreement*, Appendix C, pp. 71–2.
82. There are clear summaries in Brian Semkow, 'The legal basis of Japan's deregulation', *International Financial Law Review*, April 1985, pp. 16–19; and McRae, *Japan's Role*.
83. 'Bond underwriting still unfair, U.S. says', *Japan Economic Journal*,

30 April 1988, p. 3.

84. The major part of Frankel, *The Yen/Dollar Agreement* is taken up with these issues.
85. Wendy Cooper, 'The Financial Services Trade War', *Institutional Investor*, November 1987, pp. 117–20.
86. Rafferty, 'The assault on Article 65', *Institutional Investor*, January 1987, pp. 133–5.
87. Barry Riley, 'Snag hits Japan bid to join SE', *Financial Times*, 5 March 1986; 'Reciprocity clause worries Japan traders in London finance market', *Japan Economic Journal*, 8 November 1986, p. 4; Peter Montagnon, 'Japan may lose UK licences if 'access imbalance' remains', *Financial Times*, 20 November 1986; 'Foreign securities houses eager to expand operations', *Japan Economic Journal*, 28 March 1987, pp. 1/14.
88. Strange, *Casino Capitalism*, p. 55.
89. Adams, *Japanese Securities Markets*, p. 32.
90. Whitener, 'Japan tackles insider trading',pp. 15–18.
91. Quoted by Tatsuta, 'Enforcement of Japanese Securities Legislation', p. 112.
92. This relies on Katsuro Kanzaki, 'Developments in insider trading in Japan', *Journal of Comparative Corporate Law and Securities Regulation*' 4 (1982) pp. 391–4; and Tatsuta, 'Enforcement of Japanese Securities Legislation'.
93. Whitener, 'Japan tackles insider trading', pp. 15–18 has the figures, and material on the change in 1953.
94. Dore, 'Financial Structures and the Long-Term View'. The quotation is on p. 18. Dore's view is that this state of affairs is a contributory cause of the Japanese economic miracle. The scandalous and dis-credited stock markets, precisely because they are in this condition, can safely be ignored by industrial managers, who are thus freed to plan strategically.
95. Viner, *Inside Japan's Financial Markets*, p. 79.
96. *ibid.*
97. Dore, 'Financial Structures and the Long-Term View', p. 15.
98. From *The Economist*, 11 July 1987, p. 25.
99. Viner, *Inside Japan's Financial Markets*, pp. 67–8, 73, 217. The definition of 'Greenmail' is drawn from Valentine, *International Dictionary of the Securities Industry*, p. 88.
100. Dore, 'Financial Structures and the Long-Term View', pp. 18–19 uses the term 'AGM operators'.
101. This passage relies on: 'Firms gang up to quiet stockholder meeting louts', *Japan Economic Journal*, 2 July 1988, p. 4.
102. Whitener, 'Japan tackles insider trading', p. 16.
103. The details of the Tateho case and the 1988 measures are from: Katsumi Fujimori, 'Insider Trading', *Japan Economic Journal*, Special Survey, Summer 1988, pp. 41–2; 'Stock scandals may unravel

entwined corporate relations', *Japan Economic Journal*, 6 August 1988, pp. 1/4.

104. The story is in: 'Tougher enforcement planned', *Far Eastern Economic Review*, 15 September 1988, p. 94.

105. 'Nomura Chinese Wall sends shock to industry', *Japan Economic Journal*, 9 July 1988, p. 4; 'Institutions combat insider dealing but watchdog needs more teeth', *Japan Economic Journal*, 6 August 1988, p. 3.

106. This account is drawn from: 'New Nikkei chief emphasises integrity', *Japan Economic Journal*, 16 July 1988, pp. 1–2: 'Red-faced recruits: share scandal damages Tokyo's tax reform plans', *Far Eastern Economic Review*, 21 July 1988, pp. 17–18; 'Widening of share-profiteering case shakes government', *Far Eastern Economic Review*, 3 November 1988, p. 18.

107. Quoted, *Japan Economic Journal*, 22 October 1988, p. 4.

108. Quoted in: 'Nomura Chinese Wall sends shock waves to the industry', *Japan Economic Journal*, 9 July 1988, p. 4.

109. For instance, in the case of France see: James Lightburn, 'Insider Trading in France', *International Financial Law Review*, January 1988, pp. 23–7; and more generally, Stephen Herne, 'Inside Information: Definitions In Australia, Canada, the U.K. and the U.S.', *Journal of Comparative Business and Capital Market Law*, 8 (1986): 1–19.

110. Whitener, 'Japan tackles insider trading', p. 17.

111. Peter Alexis Gourevitch, 'Breaking with orthodoxy: the politics of economic policy responses to the Depression of the 1930s', *International Organisation*, 38 (1984): 95–129. The quotation is on p. 99.

5 States, Scandals and Financial Markets

1. Hills, *Deregulating Telecoms*.

2. Information on Baker from author's interviews with regulators. For a good instance of the general 'regulatory reform' literature see Lawrence J. White, *Reforming Regulation: Processes and Problems* (Englewood Cliffs: Prentice Hall, 1981).

3. In my interviews during 1985–86 on both sides of the Atlantic I was struck by the near universal belief in the 'reregulation' thesis among regulators and market participants.

4. There is an obvious parallel between the difficulties of creating coalitions for regulatory change and creating coalitions favouring the initial introduction of regulation. Although the substance of my argument is different, I have been influenced by the account of the conditions of coalition creation in James Q. Wilson, *The Politics of Regulation* (New York: Basic Books, 1979) pp. 366–9.

5. Zysman, *Governments, Markets and Growth*, p. 292.

6. Wyn Grant, with Jane Sargent, *Business and Politics in Britain* (London: Macmillan, 1987) chapter 2.
7. James P. Hawley, 'Protecting capital from itself: U.S. attempts to regulate the Eurocurrency system', *International Organisation*, 38 (1984): 131–65 (p. 135).
8. Eric A. Nordlinger, *On the Autonomy of the Democratic State* (Cambridge: Harvard University Press, 1981) p. 19.
9. Krasner, *Defending The National Interest*, p. 10.
10. Reid, *All-Change in the City*, pp. 52–3.
11. Krasner, *Defending the National Interest*. The first quotation is on p. 58, the second on p. 61.
12. Maurice Wright, 'Policy Community, Policy Network and Comparative Industrial Policies', *Political Studies*, vol. 36, no. 4 (1988): 593–612 (597–8).
13. G. John Ikenberry, 'The State and Strategies of International Adjustment', *World Politics*, 39 (1986): 53–77. The quotation is on p. 57.
14. On this point see Frankel, *The Yen/Dollar Agreement*, p. 2.
15. Robert W. Cox, *Production, Power, and World Order* (New York: Columbia University Press, 1987) p. 6. It should be emphasised that – as his title indicates – Cox locates structural constraints in the production structure.
16. Ibid., p. 7.
17. Ibid., pp. 359–60.
18. Ibid., pp. 399 for the first quotation and 400 for the second.
19. Strange, *States and Markets*, pp. 24–5.
20. Ibid., p. 26.
21. Ibid., p. 238.
22. On the SEC parallel see Berrill, 'Regulation in a changing City – bureaucrats and practitioners', p. 18.
23. This drive to expand jurisdiction has, since the 1970s, created a continuous debate between international securities lawyers. See: Philip A. Loomis, Jr. and Richard W. Grant, 'The U.S. Securities and Exchange Commission, Financial Institutions Outside the U.S. And Extraterritorial Application of the U.S. Securities Laws', *Journal of comparative and capital market law and securities regulation* 1 (1978): 3–38; and Peter Widmer, 'The U.S. Securities Laws – Banking Law of the World?', ibid., pp. 39–46; John M. Fedders, Friederick B. Wade, Michael D. Mann and Matthew Beizer, 'Waiver By Conduct – A Possible Response to the Internationalisation of the Securities Markets', *Journal of Comparative Business and Capital Market Law* 6 (1984) 1–54; the responses by a range of lawyers in the special issue of the same journal, December 1984; and S. Martin, 'The Fedders Proposal Won't Go Away', *Euromoney*, April 1985, pp. 45–9.
24. See J. Warner, 'New Act could cost City 100 million', *The Independent*, 4 June 1987, quoting a study by David Lomax.
25. For a scathing and convincing analysis of the 'elaborate and empty'

body of jurisprudence governing insider dealing see Michael P. Dooley, 'Enforcement of Insider Trading Restrictions', *Virginia Law Review*, 66 (1980): 1–83.

26. Vogel, *National Styles of Regulation*, p. 267.
27. See Friedman and Schwartz, *A Monetary History of the United States*, pp. 113–19.
28. Burns, *The American Banking Community and New Deal Banking Reforms*, is an authoritative study.
29. Hugh Heclo, 'Issue Networks and the Executive Establishment', in Anthony King (ed.), *The New American Political System* (Washington: American Enterprise Institute, 1978) pp. 87–124. The quotation is on p. 102.
30. Vogel, *National Styles of Regulation*, pp. 250–1.
31. Edward A. Shils, *The torment of secrecy: the background and consequences of American security policies* (Glencoe: Free Press, 1956).
32. Hall, *Governing the Economy*, p. 262.
33. Strange, *States and Markets*, p. 117.

Index